ETHNIC DANCES AND MUSIC OF WESTERN ORISSA

About the Author

Dr. Bhagyalaxmi Mahapatra, is an alumni of Khalikote Autonomous College, Berhampur and had completed her M.Sc. in Anthropology in 1984. An educationist by profession, she had done B.Ed., followed by Diploma in Computers and had teaching experience in various schools in Delhi, Hyderabad and Wellington. She was awarded Ph.D. in Anthropology in the year 2004 by the Berhampur University on the "Didayi", a primitive tribal group of Orissa.

Subsequently, she had pursued her research career in the Council of Analytical Tribal Studies (COATS), Koraput, Orissa, a Project Fellow in UGC sponsored Project in Government College, Phulbani, Orissa. Now she is a Senior Fellow under Ministry of Culture, Government of India.

Dr. Bhagyalaxmi is now running a NGO named ASPIRE (Action for Socio-Economic Progress in Rural Environment) and working with a Motto—"Aspire to Inspire" for the development of women, youths and children of Orissa.

Currently working as a State Level Trainer in the State Institute of Rural Development (SIRD) of Government of Orissa, she has been imparting capacity building training to the PRIs of Orissa.

Ethnic Dances and Music of Western Orissa

An Anthropological Study Towards Promoting Eco-Tourism

Dr. Bhagyalaxmi Mahapatra

CONCEPT PUBLISHING COMPANY PVT. LTD.
NEW DELHI-110 059

The publication was financially supported by the ICSSR. The responsibility for the facts stated, opinions expressed or conclusions reached is entirely that of the author and the ICSSR accepts no responsibility for them.

The work was evaluated by Professor S.M. Dubey, Former Professor of Sociology & Social Anthropology, Dibrugarh University, Assam, on behalf of the ICSSR.

ISBN-13 : 978-81-8069-741-8

First Published 2011

Published and Printed by

Concept
Since 1974

Concept Publishing Company Pvt. Ltd.
Regd. Office :
A/15-16, Commercial Block, Mohan Garden
New Delhi-110059 (India)
Phones : 25351460, 25351794, *Fax :* 091-11-25357109
Email : publishing@conceptpub.com
Website : www.conceptpub.com

Editorial Office :
H-13, Bali Nagar, New Delhi-110 015, India.

Cataloging in Publication Data--*Courtesy:* D.K. Agencies (P) Ltd. <docinfo@dkagencies.com>

Mahapatra, Bhagyalaxmi.
Ethnic dances and music of western Orissa : an anthropological study towards promoting eco-tourism / Bhagyalaxmi Mahapatra.
p. cm.
Includes bibliographical references (p.) and index.
ISBN 9788180697418

1. Folk dancing--India--Kalahandi (District) 2. Folk dance music--India--Kalahandi (District) 3. Ecotourism--India--Kalahandi (District) I. Title.

DDC 793.31954133 22

Foreword

Tourism in a number of States has become the major sector which has led to significant growth in income and employment. Each State with tourism potential has tried to highlight and take advantage of the natural and cultural heritage through attractive forms of packaging. The uniqueness of a particular natural and cultural factor has been adequately emphasized to attract tourists.

That Orissa has tremendous tourism potential is undeniable. So far, we have been able to harness only a small fraction of it. The ethnic dimension in the broad sense should actually be given maximum attention. Because eco-tourism in the upland region of Orissa generates a number of forms, it can at the same time promote conservation of natural resources, bio-diversity, etc. besides many economic benefits.

In this context, the comprehensive study by Dr. Bhagyalaxmi Mahapatra of how ethnic dances and music of Western Orissa can be used as a vibrant medium of development of tourism is of great value since it brings to light the factors which influence the functioning of these cultural forms. It brings out the tremendous variety of folk dances and music which is argument for developing eco-tourism in Western Orissa in a viable manner. I do hope the study is seriously taken by folk scholars, policy-makers and administrators. I congratulate Dr. Mahapatra for carrying out such a comprehensive study in a relatively unexplored yet important area.

S.P. Padhi
Director Incharge
(NKCDS), C.S. Pur
Bhubaneswar-13

Acknowledgements

I am thankful to Indian Council of Social Science Research (ICSSR, New Delhi) for financial aid.

I would like to express my sincere gratitude to Prof. Shakti Padhi, Director of the NKCDS for his cooperation and administrative support for the successful completion of this Project.

I am grateful to Dr. P.K. Acharya, Reader in Social Anthropology, NKCDS, for his humble guidance and motivation.

I am thankful to the Administrative Officer, Mr. Srikanta Ratha for rendering his timely necessary official support. I also express my sincere regards to Dr. R.K. Mahapatra, Librarian, for his cooperation.

I take this opportunity to convey my regards to Mr. Jaganath Sahu, Research Assistant, and Mr. Lalitendu Mahapatra, Research Investigator for their strenuous fieldwork in the remote areas of the Kalahandi district. I am also thankful to Mrs. Jyotirmayee Mishra for her computer assistance.

I am indebted to all the resource persons and informants for their cooperation and support.

I am solely responsible for the views expressed here or for any errors therein.

Bhagyalaxmi Mahapatra

Contents

List of Tables

List of Maps, Graphs and Figures

List of Maps

List of Graphs

List of Figures

List of Photographs

List of Abbreviations

AIR	All India Radio
BPL	Below Poverty Line
CRZ	Coastal Regulation Zone
CSD	Commission on Sustainable Development
DA	Dearness Allowance
DHQ	District Head Quarters
GP	Gram Panchayat
FGD	Focus Group Discussion
IYE	International Year of Eco-tourism
KBK	Kalahandi, Bolangir and Koraput districts
KKD	Kutia Kandh Development Agency
MFP	Minor Forest Produce
MPCE	Monthly Per Capita Consumer Expenditure
NAP	National Action Plan
NCAER	National Council of Applied Economic Research
NCT	National Committee on Tourism
NGO	Non-Governmental Organization
NREGS	National Rural Employment Generating Scheme
NSS	National Sample Survey
PRA	Participating Rural Appraisal Method
PTGs	Primitive Tribal Group
RTI	Right to Information Act
SCP	Special Connective Programme
TA	Travel Allowance
UNICEF	United Nations International Children's Emergency Fund
UNEP	United Nations Environment Programme
VSS	Vana Surakhya Samiti
WTO	World Trade Organization
WTTC	World Travel and Tourism Council

1

Introduction

India with its vast variety of ethnicity is a veritable storehouse of folk dances and music. No other single culture perhaps can boast of such a huge variety of ethnic music and dances as our country can. In India, the core category of ethnic identity is based on a sense of peoplehood which constitutes caste, religion, region and languages. Ethnicity is based on the 'we' feelings, shared by the members of a group that ultimately lead to an ethnic pluralism. Even, our Constitution encourages and guarantees this ethnic pluralism. On the other hand it discourages ethnic disparity, terrorism, movements, violences, clashes etc.

The principle of ethnicity has been recognized as one of the important factors in administration and development process during the colonial and post-colonial periods in terms of (a) recognition of certain communities as backward, tribals, or in modern parlances as ethics, (b) drawing the ethnic boundaries, and (c) imparting a bias to policy and programmes to provide protection and ensure development of these ethnic communities (Singh, 1990 : 31-41). In fact ethnicity is an excellent tool for identification of the aspirations of a community. Its limitations and its core identity.

According to Narayan (1989) an ethnic group is a self-pertinent group of people who hold in a common set of cultural traditions, not shared with others with whom they are in contact. However, while defining ethnicity, it is necessary to make a distinction between the symbols of cultural boundaries which are transmitted from one generation to another as these symbols represent an ethnic group. Furthermore, an ethnic group can be called as a folk group with at least some linking factors such as common occupation, language, religion and cultural traditions which are being transmitted since generations. As Pasayat (1998) has defined folk as a distinct group with three categories : (1) sharing a culture; (2) group identity in terms of culture; and (3) regional identity in terms of culture. According to Redfield (1947 : 293-308) there is synonymity between primitive and folk cultures. Again he says that the characteristic of a folk typology in most ways corresponds to that of a tribal ethnic group.

Ethnic dance and music are like two sides of a coin compatible to each other. Both of them symbolize an indegenous folk tradition which represents a genre of performing art of a specific cultural area. Moreover, the rich tradition of music and dance of both classical and folk forms, together inexplicably add further richness to the cultural heritage of India.

Orissa, located on the eastern part of the country, is surrounded by Andhra Pradesh, Chhattisgarh, Jharkhand and West Bengal. The climate and rainfall of the State is influenced by the Bay of Bengal in the east. It has an area about 155,782 sq.km. distributed under 30 districts, 58 subdivisions, 171 tahsils, 314 CD Blocks and 368.05 lakh population (Census, 2001).

Orissa is stupendously rich in its folk heritage in spite of its typical geographical features like the coastal belts, hilly terrain and scenic mountain slopes. It has been noticed that rural and tribal people of its respective regions, i.e. East, West, North and South, have their distinctive folk culture and traditions. Broadly speaking, folk dance and music of Orissa can be categorized as according to the ethnicity of the respective region. The present study justifies its importance by trying to make a critical appraisal of the folk dance and music of Western Orissa as well as its significance in promoting eco-tourism in the region. It has been found that few tourist spots of Kalahandi district have been shown in Orissa Tourist Map (Map 1.1).

The present chapter has six inter-related sections. The first section describes the problem. The second section covers an

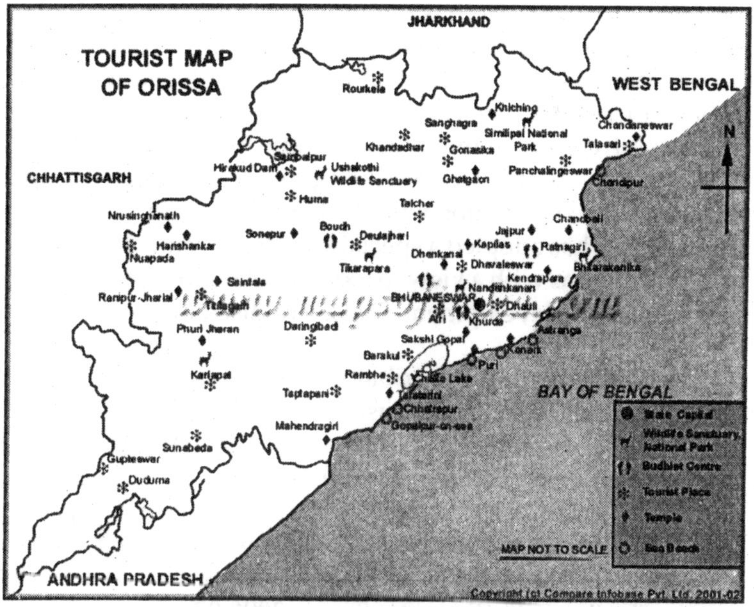

Map 1.1 : Tourist Map of Orissa

overview of literature. The third section presents a conceptual framework. The fourth section deals with the hypothesis. The fifth section mentions the objectives of the study. The last section presents a brief idea about the anatomy of the study, which includes study area, methods and techniques employed, sampling/sample size, survey design, and chapterisation of the study.

Statement of the Problem

Western Orissa has many typical forms of folk dance and music which are not found elsewhere in the State. Although, the ten districts comprising Western Orissa have a common folk tradition, each district has its own distinct speciality in the arena of folk dance and music owing to the tribal and rural concentration. It is, therefore, essential to identify the distinctions between each traditional art form of the corresponding area so that, the study will be the area specific and authentic.

Western Orissa is considered as one of the most backward poverty stricken and drought prone region of the State. The Government of India has formed a special Project namely, KBK Project for revival of socio-economic conditions of eight KBK districts of Orissa, namely Kalahandi, Nuapada, Bolangir, Subarnapur, Koraput, Malkangiri, Nabarangpur and Rayagada. In consultation with the Government of India, State Government has adopted a special area development approach for these regions with a view to focus greater attention on them for accelerated development. These are discussed as below :

- Demographically, tribal communities dominate this region (38.41% : Census, 2001). KBK region is perhaps the poorest region in the country with highest incidence of poverty (*Economic Survey 2006-07*). According to the report of the committee on the constitution of separate Development Board in Orissa, 96 per cent of CD Blocks in these districts are either "very backward" or "backward" (*Economic Survey 2006-07*).
- The old Koraput and Kalahandi districts and portions of Bolangir districts are mainly hilly. Because of these factors severe droughts and floods often visit to the region. Due to recurrent droughts and lack of employment, the people of these regions migrate to other neighbouring States, namely Andhra Pradesh and Madhya Pradesh.
- Apart from that the KBK districts are rich in forest resources with NTFP, medicinal plants, wildlife, natural fountains and rivers. On the other hand, these resources have not yet received adequate investments and appropriate managerial inputs over the time. (*Economic Survey 2006-07*).
- These districts with greater concentration of tribal and rural population, are endowed with enriched folk traditions and culture.
- If there can be upgradation of eco-tourism in the regions, it will not only attract the tourists throughout the year but also enhance the economic status of local

folk mass and retention of the surrounding hills and mountains. Furthermore, it will also check the migration practices.

Overview of Literature

There is paucity of literature on folk dance, folk music and folk culture of people of Western Orissa. However, there have been a few anthropological as well as the relevant studies on the folk dance and music of Orissa.

Naik (2000 : 34-41) opines that old and archic culture are not only considered to have their respective values but themselves are valuable resources that could be tapped for betterment of people and economic development of the State. He further states that cultures are considered not merely having preservative values but having a great deal of investment values. He has made another important observation with regard to utilization of traditional resources. Further he has reiterated that controlled eco-tourism could be allowed to specific areas and villages where proper natural-cultural arrangements could be made to facilitate both tourism and selling of crafts and commodities of local people.

Scholars like Mahanti and Sahoo (2000 : 22-23) have given the significance of music as a popular medium for the propagation of social feelings and values. Further giving significance of music, they have stated that music can be played through instrument for educating the community men and pleasure the outsiders. Hence, it functions as a proper medium for the propagation of social feelings and values.

As Singh (2007) mentions that proper survey and analysis of folk dances of any area is only possible if we understand the existence of different folk-circles of that respective area constituting caste, region, religion and historical bases of those circles in right context. At the same time, we have to keep the fact in our minds that for related folklore, there is always a continuous flow of dynamic changes between cultural genres. He describes that after partition the present form of folk dances especially *Bhangra* and *Giddha* of Punjab are accepted as the authentic form. Although, these folk dances gained importance currently as performing form of stage art but in reality, from historical point of view, they have come a long way from folk performance and folk elements of their folk circles. Hence, it is improper and out of context to position the current form of these folk dances as their original form. He further illustrates through examples of folk dances of Punjab that authentication of folk dance is determined through its folk-tradition, that tradition which while residing with its folk is under a process of continuous transformation. That is how any dance can be understood in historical context from the available contemporary forms. That is why, while analyzing any folk dance and music, the study of art, aesthetic sense, music and dramaturgy are prerequisite and also important.

Generally, tribal folk songs and dances are found connoted with festive occasions, feats and merry making. Further, these traditional folk songs and dances are orally handed down from generation to generation in absence of any scripts among the indigenous people (Tayang, 1990).

Bhatta and Bhargava (2005), while looking into the folk sprits of some neighbouring States, namely Bihar, Jharkhand, Chhattisgarh and Madhya Pradesh, have expressed that both the tribal and the rural folk of these States observe indigenous folk practices, namely song, dance and music. According to them folk dance and music are the integral part of their social interaction which they have cited through various folk practices of these neighbouring States. For example, the tribal communities of Jharkhand while observing *sarhul* festival, worship the sal tree with dance, music, drinking and camaraderie. Likewise, they practise *Chhau* dance for which they use tattoo painting and mask. In Madhya Pradesh the *Gaur* dance of the Sing Marias or bison-horned Marias, is one of the most popular dances. This dance symbolizes the hunting spirit of the tribe of Madhya Pradesh and accompanied with various instruments. Besides there are various dances, namely *Muria* dance, *Saila* dance, *Karma* dance, *Kaksar* dance etc. Generally, all these dances are associated with rhythm and melody. Again while mentioning about Chhattisgarh, they have made their observations that the State has its own folk dance styles, music and traditional folk songs in which *sohar, bihav* and *pathoni* songs are very famous. In the region the most popular dances are *Pandwani Nach, Raut Nach, Panthi* and *Soowa* dance styles.

Another scholar Hasnain (2007) has opined that Bihar occupies a very important place in 'Tribal India'. According to him the Chotanagpur plateau constitutes a tribal belt of some of the largest tribal inhabitants of the country, namely Oraon, Munda, Ho, Santhal, Kharia, Pahariya and Birhor. These tribals are well-known for Jharkhand movement and for their traditional folk dance. The *Chau*, popularly known as masked dance, is one of the unique folk dances of Bihar and is found to be still preserved by the royal family of the former state of Saraikela in Bihar. A Chau dancer impersonates a God, animal, bird, hunter, rainbow, or flower through his mask. Generally, it is performed at the annual *Chaitra Parva* festival. Also in Orissa it is practised in different form that is without a mask, in Mayurbhanj district.

As Pasayat (1998) overviews that folk mass though illiterate are by nature quick composers. The words used for composition of folk music, dance and drama are natural but full of figurative literary styles and moreover can be sung with rhythm. Again he states that folk songs and drama contain various sentiments and nature for which the source of inspirations are trees, birds, sky etc. Apart from that many social and economic aspects are also reflected in the folk songs, dances and dramas such as social relationship, marital relationship, etc. Even the tunes, rhythms, costumes, instruments and make-up used are conceived by the folk mass and prepared mostly from indigenous and locally available material.

Another scholar Panigrahi (1998) observes that although *Ghumra* dance is found in Sonepur, Bolangir and Kalahandi districts, the dance form is most popular in Kalahandi district. Regarding the *Dhaap Nritya* he has mentioned that the dance is in dying state despite its popularity.

Mahapatra (2000) justifies that Orissa culture is a by-product of the ancient tribal and folk culture inclusive of performing arts like music, dance and theatre, which are the basic tenets of folk tradition. According to him the most significant features of folk dance and music are (a) absence of fixed grammar, (b) absence of documentation, (c) oral transmission from person to person, generation-wise and, (d) spontaneity and freedom for improvisations during the performance itself.

Kalahandi which once was synonymous with drought, backwardness, hunger, death etc., which was known as a land where the pot (*handi*) was not getting black (*kala*) due to lack of foodgrains, has once again earned a good fame throughout the world as a pot of art (Kalahandi) and most of the credit goes to the *Ghumra* dance (Kumar, 2002).

True to the fact that judicial and planned exploitation of local resources in any form, i.e. natural, material or cultural form, is the basic premise for ensuring a really sustainable development of a region. Hence, folkdance and music forms of Western Orissa, can altogether be the most suitable growth engine of the region under the National Tourism Policy (2002) that lays emphasis on the segments such as heritage, tourism, rural tourism and eco-tourism.

Conceptual Framework

History and Evolution of Folkdance and Music

It may be viewed that folk culture is the predominant feature of the folk society while recognizing the possible existence of certain elements of folk culture in other societal types such as urban, rural, primitive, peasant and the like (Oomen, 2001). According to Dunde (1965 : 2) the term folk can refer to any group of people who share at least one common linking factor with a common core of traditional identity. It can be said that both the categories of folk and ethnic, are not distinct from each other. For example, a peasant group of a particular culture area can produce a folk culture of its own. There may be a number of peasant groups with varied social, cultural and regional backgrounds but all these groups can be pulled under a single category of folk. Similarly, the tribal culture of a particular area can be treated as folk culture. Likewise, the area of a folk culture embraces the total way of life or ethnicity to its fold.

Since time immemorial music and dance together have remained as a medium of self-expression. Folk songs are remarkable for their brooding sweetness, long drawn out melody and luxuriant imaginative experiences. Rhythmic folk dance connotes the force of verse, the beauty of expression, and scintillating chain of similes and metaphors which on the whole left a long lasting memorable impression on the spectators through the combined effect of the melody, rhythm and harmony. The most significant features of folk dance and music are : (a) absence of fixed grammar usages, (b) absence of documentation, (c) oral transmission from person to person or generation to generation, and (d) spontaneity or flexibility of action by the performers during the performances. In true sense, it is 'By the people' and 'For the people'. Both of these art forms constitute the integral part of the culture of the rural ethnic group. Each of these groups has its own ethnic identity and distinct cultural pattern that comprises folk lores, folk arts, music, dance etc. Tribal or folk literature is mainly based on their folk songs that passed from generation to generation. The tribal or folk literature displays traditions as well as changes.

The primitive man in his own awakened thought could clearly see that life manifests itself in rhythm. Heart beat, breathing, walking, all these signs of a living body are basically rhythmic. The difference between a living and a dead is that while the former has rhythm within itself, that latter has none. Man soon realized that only some rhythmic activities could bring him certain momentary celebration. His reasoning power spontaneously guided him to be engaged in dance and music long before he learnt speaking some kind of dialect. Many scholars are, therefore, of the opinion that dance is the mother of all arts.

The tribal and non-tribal people like to dance not only for the sake of entertaining the audiences but also to celebrate life in full spirits. These celebrating dances are known as folk dances and the sophisticated highly evolved art dances as classical.

Towards a Definition of Folk Dance, Folk Music and Folk Song

The terms folk song, folk music, and folk dance are said to be the extensions of the term folklore.These are reflected as the traditions, customs, and superstitions of the uncultured classes. Again it is said that these terms are derived from the German expression *'volk'* which connotes the people as a whole (Thomas, 1846).

Scholars and dancers further differ in what they admit under the level of folk dance. One may see folk dance as the traditional dances of a country that evolve spontaneously from the everyday activities and experiences of its people. Another may define it as embracing only dances with magical and economical functions, or those that are performed for all non-professional reasons.

The term folk music originated in the nineteenth century as a term for musical folklore. It has been defined in several ways; as music of the lower classes, music with no known composer since the middle of the twentieth century the term has also been used to describe a kind of popular music that is based on traditional music (*Encyclopedia Wikipedia*).

The Technical Multimedia Music Dictionary defines folk music as "music of the common people that has been passed on by memorization or repetitions rather than by writing and has deep roots in its own culture." According to Webster's Dictionary, folk music is the "traditional and typical anonymous music that is an expressive of life of the people in a community".

Seegar (1980) describes three contemporary defining criteria of folk music :

1. A scheme is comprising of four musical types : 'primitive' or 'tribal', 'elite' or 'art', 'folk' or 'popular'.

Usually, folk music is associated with a lower class societies which are culturally and socially stratified;
2. "Cultural processes rather than abstract music types"; and
3. Less prominent, "a rejection of rigid boundaries, preferring a conception, simply of varying practices within one field, that of music".

It is a noteworthy factor that folk music is easily identified with the ordinary working people who creates it, and preserve these as the most treasured things against the claimed relentless encroachments of capitalism. Furthermore, it is seen that although the movies and pop music have weakened folk music's popularity, but at the same time these cheaply recordable items facilitate revival of old traditions.

Folklore

Folklore is the literature of the people that includes folk music and songs. Folklore represents a significant folk culture, which is enriched with indigenous resources. These resources in the long run process of cross-cultured contact, give new elements to cultures.

Nature and Function of Folk Dance

Many folk dances best reveal their ancient functions when performed in their native habitat. Outside this context, in a school of gymnasium or a stage, they lose their aura, but inside village they enhance spirit of communication, consciousness and brotherhood. Notwithstanding the trend towards sociable and theatrical objective, many folk dances celebrate original festivals. Taking the example of American countries, they show many adjustments to the Christian feasts. In Austria and many European countries, they dance for renewed vegetation.

Indian folk dance is diverse because of India's vast cultural diversity. Again, here, according to the nature and functions, the vast body of folk dances can be further subdivided according to the basic character or particular occasion of performance of dance.

In India, the range and variety of folk dance traditions surviving in India is indeed amazing. The subcontinent has around thirty different cultural regions. In each there are scores of differing styles of folk dance. The vast body of folk traditions can be mainly divided into two categories : dances performed by the tribal communities, and those by the non-tribal communities. The tribal dances are either ritualistic or simple celebrative. The folk people on the other hand, have two kinds of dance traditions : performs for the audience and the other does not presuppose any audience.

The vast body of Indian folk dances can be further sub-divided according to the basic character or particular occasion of performance of the dance. Such as ritual dances, trance dances, ceremonial dances, harvest dances, social dances, seasonal dances, marital and game dances, dances of boys as girls, drum dances and recreational dances.

Forms and Techniques

Although, attendance at public fiestas is haphazard, the participants in many dance gatherings observe closely knit organization and definite rules for the individual's place in the community and in the communal dances. Take for example the European combat dances where the performers belong to a sworn brotherhood of ancient origin. Similar patterns can also be observed among the Indian folk performers.

Styles of Movement

Function, sex and age all have an effect on a dancer's style of movement. Other psychological factors of group and individual temperament and mood have, for untold centuries, determined the quality and the type of steps and gestures. The climate and topography may have had an effect on the development of regional styles.

Evolutionary Trend

The evolutionary process in the relation between the dance and other arts, is very similar to the development of the dance itself. From total integration of dance and life in the rural to the modern rock'n roll, there are many factors—the passage of centuries, the change from animism to Christianity, the shift from hunting to agriculture, and handicrafts to industrialization. Moreover, the emergence of popular folk artists began during the twentieth century which brought a crucial change in the history of folk music.

India has been witnessing various ethnic movements which has been caused for the formation of new States, new political parties, scripts etc. such as Jharkhand, Chhattisgarh and Uttarakhand States, Jharkhand Mukti Morcha, Santali scripts, and acculturation of folk traditions. The most underlying factor behind these movements is ethnocentrism where there is unique value and rightness for one's own group and its way of life.

The folk music and songs are known as best accompaniment to the folk dancer. First, it is probably one of the most ancient form of accompaniment because of its independent form. Second, it is aesthetically pleasing. Finally, the songs have text of historical, sociological, or ecological importance.

Concept of Eco-tourism

Background of the International Year of Eco-tourism

The United Nations General Assembly, by its resolution A/Res/53/200, proclaimed the year 2002 as the International Year of Eco-tourism (IYE). The Seventh session of the Commission on Sustainable Development (CSD) held in New York in April 1999 gave a mandate to the World Tourism Organization (WTO) and the United Nations Environment Programme (UNEP) to assume the responsibility for the IYE, and adopted a resolution inviting Governments, the UN and NGOs to organize activities for celebration of IYE.

The term "eco-tourism" seems to have a definition for everyone. In a generalized term, the definition of eco-tourism boils down to a special form of tourism that meets three criteria : (1) It provides for conservation measures; (2) It includes meaningful community participation; and (3) It is profitable and can sustain itself. However, these three components of eco-tourism are difficult to accomplish individually as they are difficult to measure or quantity.

According to UNEP, Eco-tourism as development tool can advance the three basic goals of the convention on Biological Diversity :

- Conserve biological and cultural diversity by strengthening protected area management systems both public and private sectors and enhance the value of sound eco-system;
- Promote the sustainable use of bio-diversity, by generating income, jobs, business opportunities in eco-tourism and related business networks; and
- Share the benefits of eco-tourism development equitably with local community and indigenous people, by obtaining their informed consent and active participation in both planning and management of eco-tourism business.

Principles

According to Quebec Declaration on Eco-tourism, eco-tourism embraces the principles of sustainable tourism which are stated as below :

- Contributes actively to the conservation of natural and cultural heritage.
- Includes local and indigenous communities in its planning, development and operation contributing to their well-being.
- Interprets the natural and cultural heritage of the destination to visitor.
- Lends itself better to independent travellers, as well as to organized tour for small groups.

Guidelines

In May 2002, on the eighth session of the United Nations Commission on Sustainable Development (CSD), a group of indigenous people's organizations, NGOs and other members of civil society provided a proposal on guidelines for eco-tourism. The UNEP recognized these guidelines which overviews eco-tourism as sustainable tourism involving a continuous process :

- Ensures prior informed participants of all stakeholders.
- Ensures equal, effective and active participation of all stakeholders.
- Acknowledges indigenous people's communities rights to say "no" to tourism development and to be fully informed, effective and active participants in the development of tourism activities within the communities, lands and territories.
- Promotes processes of indigenous people and local communities to control and maintain their resources.

Official Launching of IYE

The official launching ceremony of the International year of Eco-tourism 2002 took place at the United Nations Headquarters in New York on 28th January, 2002. The text proclaiming 2002 as the International Year of Eco-tourism referred specially to Agenda 21 adopted in Rio in 1992 under which it states the basic objectives of sustainable development in less developed countries. Several Government Ministers, representatives of inter-governmental organizations, members of diplomatic corps on UN, and representatives of leading industrial associations and NGOs attended the event.

The agenda for the IYE 2002 was passed with four objectives in mind which are :

(1) Generate greater awareness among the public authority, private sector, the civil society and consumers regarding the eco-tourism's capacity to

contribute to the conservation of the natural and cultural heritage in natural and rural areas, and the improvement of standards of living in these areas.

(2) Disseminate methods and techniques for the planning, management regulative and monitoring of eco-tourism to guarantee its long-term sustainability.

(3) Promote exchange of successful experiences in the field of eco-tourism.

(4) Increase opportunities for the efficient marketing and promotion of eco-tourism destinations and products on international markets.

Quebec Declaration

The Eco-tourism summit was the principal event to mark 2002 as the International Year of Eco-tourism. Under the initiation of WTO and UNEP, it was hoisted by Tourism Quebec and Canadian Tourism Commission. The main outcome of the Summit is the Quebec Declaration 'On Eco-tourism', a document that was prepared through wide consultation at the summit and contains general guidelines, as well as states specific recommendations for sustainable development of eco-tourism. The following are the principles, which distinguish it from the wider concept of sustainable tourism :

- Contributes actively to the conservation of natural and cultural heritage.
- Includes local and indigenous communities in its planning, development and operation contributing to their well-being.
- Interprets the natural and cultural heritage of the destination to visitor.
- Lends itself better to independent travellers, as well as to organize tour for small groups.

Eco-tourism Activities

The information on eco-tourism related activities throughout the IYE and WTO Tourism Market Trends, 2002 survey has been obtained through a specific worldwide survey conducted by WTO and National Tourism Authority between January 2003 to May 2003. The information received on national and local activities carried out the framework of the IYE based on the certain themes, which are as under :

- National Policy;
- Activities and publications;
- Stakeholders participation and support;
- Awareness;
- Regulation; and
- Cooperation.

Eco-tourism in India

The fast growing tourism industry in India has witnessed a paradigm shift from conventional tourism to eco-tourism. This change owes basically to outflows of tourists and consequent adverse ecological impact and implications to the host region. Eco-tourism in India combines the pleasure of discovering spectacular flora, fauna, archaeological monuments, historical monuments, natural scenic views and pilgrimages. At the same time, it provides opportunity to maintain a balance between conservation and development in order to check the disruption in the eco-system and despoliation of archaeological monuments, etc. A National Committee on Tourism (NCT) was set up by Planning Commission in July 1986 to evolve a plan. The Committee submitted its report in 1988 that emphasizes on low-cost economy, higher levels of productivity, improvement in efficiency of infrastructure and promoting competition. In May 1992, the Government of India under Eighth Five Year Plan formulated the NAP (National Action Plan) for Tourism, that gave priority on private initiation through the respective State Government's intervention and also on creation of Special Tourist Areas. According to the report of the World Travel and Tourism Council (WTTC), India has the potential to generate 25 million additional jobs in the Tourism sector by 2010. The Government of India in November 1982, for the first time announced its Tourism Policy.

Subsequently, the policy recognized the importance of international tourism in earning foreign exchange.

Eco-tourism's Risk and Benefits

Eco-tourism can have both positive and negative effect on an area's eco-system, economy and culture.

Eco-tourism allows visitors to learn about the environment of an area while maintaining the environment's pristine state. The money generated from eco-tourism usually returns to the local community rather than going to distant companies or corporations.

However, there are some disadvantages to eco-tourism in the long run. It is true that with other forms of tourism, a community's culture and ethnicity can be influenced by the impact of the outsiders visiting the area.

Hypothesis

Specific questions, which are expected to be answered by the study, are formulated and enumerated for the study are as under :

- Varieties of folk dance and music of Western Orissa are in dying state.
- Socio-economic state of folk mass of Western Orissa is poor.
- The folk arts and folk artisans encounter many problems while practicing their art form.
- Incentives awarded by government/NGOs for promotion of cultural forms as well as the well-being of artists are not adequate.

Objectives

The study has adopted eight objectives under which the entire processes of data collection and analysis have been made :

(i) To explore the varieties of folk dance and music both in the past and present in Western Orissa.
(ii) To study the socio-economic condition of the folk artisans.
(iii) To find out the problems and hindrances faced by the performers towards achieving excellence.
(iv) To suggest ways and means for development of ethnic art, dance and music towards formulating appropriate cultural policy.
(v) To assume the potentialities and feasibility of organizing the troupes and integrating them in the national and international sphere.
(vi) To identify eco-friendly tourist destinations in the regions for attracting outsiders around the year.
(vii) To find out the strategies towards educating and raising awareness about social problems among the mass through folk dance and music.
(viii) To suggest ways and means for facilitating ethnic dance and music for promotion of eco-tourism.

Methods Adopted for Study

Coverage of the Study

Western Orissa is very rich in terms of folk dance and music since it comprises an admixture of social groups of Chhattisgarh, Madhya Pradesh, Andhra Pradesh, Bihar and Coastal Orissa. It offers an unique opportunity to delineate natives and their horizontal cultural traditions along with the synthetic culture of Western Orissa.

Western Orissa comprises ten districts, i.e. Kalahandi, Deogarh, Jharsuguda, Nuapada, Baragada, Bolangir, Boudh, Sambalpur, Sundargarh and Subarnapur. These districts were carved out from erstwhile four major districts such as Kalahandi, Bolangir, Sambalpur and Sundargarh in 1992. The culture and tradition being followed in these four districts depict the general pattern of the entire region. Out of ten districts, Kalahandi happens to be prominent and significant.

Kalahandi is widely known for its famine and starvation. The Government of India has made a special project, namely KBK (Koraput, Bolangir, Kalahandi) for reviving its socio-economic condition.

Due to lack of employment, the people migrate to other neighbouring States like Madhya Pradesh, Andhra Pradesh, Chhattisgarh etc. in search of livelihood. If there can be upgradation of eco-tourism in the region, it will not only bring economic enhancement of the folk masses but also check massive migration.

Historically, Kalahandi district was a princely state and known for its folk art, dance, drama and music. The artisans used to be patronized by the prince's family. Since independence, owing to the lack of patronization and shift of government's attention to other problems of the region these art forms are withering.

As a source of viable entertainment, particularly in the festive occasions, the folk dance and music not only enriches the traditions and the history, but also bind different ethnic groups together for enhancing social harmony and solidarity.

Kalahandi is rich in natural resources, historical monuments, cultural heritage and archaeological excavations. Considering all these potential factors as the sustainable source of eco-tourism, the present study has explored Kalahandi district and also taken into account as the universe of the study.

Study Area

The study required total comprehension of folk dance and music as well as the promotion of eco-tourism through these folk culture and tradition. As per the strategic requirement the study further followed the classification of area into different cultural zones depending on the concentration/distribution of the folk artisans/performers. Besides, other potential factors promoting eco-tourism were also given due importance. Each zone was empirically was covered for gathering the first hand information on these diacritical marks as well as cultural traits of the sites.

The district Kalahandi is a repository of three types of tourism : (a) Eco-Tourism, (b) Cultural Tourism, and (c) Religious Tourism. Hence, the study required a total coverage of all the cultural sites for the total comprehension of tradition, ethnic arts, especially dance and music.

Sample Design

The sample for the study was designed to be as viable and representative as possible. The Kalahandi district has thirteen Blocks out of which six Blocks, namely—Bhawanipatna, Dharmagarh, Koksara, Lanjigarh, Narla and Thuamul Rampur were selected as the sample Blocks (Map 1.2).

Map 1.2 : Kalahandi District and the Sample Blocks

The present study was conducted considering the various factors such as composition of ethnic population, ecological surroundings, socio-economic status, age group composition, distance from district headquarters, communication facilities, cultural factors, impact of industrialisation and modernization. Prior to the primary data collection, a pilot study was conducted to determine the information regarding location, distribution and identification of the folk artists of the undertaken six Blocks using secondary sources, namely—respective cultural organization of the Block, District cultural organization of Bhawanipatna (Government), and Mahavira Sanskrutika Anushthana. Besides, additional information on avenues for eco-tourism and folk dance which have been recorded are used as conceptual tools and guiding factors for the present study. These inputs have also been mentioned in the desirable manner in the respective chapter. During the study the primary and secondary data, as well as qualitative and quantitative data have been taken into account. Further, looking at the requirement the study has attributed to various resource methods such as troop's member, individual household survey, case study, PRA method and focused discussion with an intention of exploring the objective of the study. The findings of the study have been incorporated in the following chapters.

Sources of Data Collection/Techniques of Data Collection

For the purpose of the present study, the techniques and tools employed for the collection of the primary data, were based on observation (participant and non-participant) to gather the information on respective folk dance and its troupe's activities. The said method was also followed to collect the information on social, economic and cultural way of life of the folk dancers. Besides, interview, schedules and case studies were also documented. Apart from that, the opinion surveys were conducted by administering a pair of structured schedules.

Furthermore, data from secondary sources such as official records, research literatures, were also used for the study. According to the requirement, the unconventional techniques, namely—PRA methods and focused group discussion methods were also used to gather information and insight from the government and non-government officials, local traders, hoteliers, businessmen, folk artist and artisans. Discussions were also held with various research persons of Kalahandi district who have been associated with the promotional part of art, culture, tourism and heritage of the district. Their viewpoints on promoting eco-tourism through folk dance and music were also recorded. Simultaneously, utmost care was taken to make the people as well as the stakeholders to understand the research objectives, planning and implementation mechanism as well as its after effects.

Sample Size

In order to record the views and counterviews of the local population two sets of structured schedule ; one exclusively for folk artists/performers and other for the elite groups (administrators, local traders, businessmen, hoteliers and transport operators) were formulated. These schedules were used as canvassing tools for collecting empirical data on socio-economic conditions of the folk artists and the viewpoints of the people in the stakeholders relating to the hindrances as well as prospective of eco-tourism in the area. Data from the secondary sources such as district cultural office, forest department, village/district/State cultural committees, voluntary cultural organizations (Mahavir Sanskrutika Anusthana) and Western Orissa Development Council were collected.

Based on the above discussed research objective two sets of schedules have been framed so that these issues could be analysed with proper interpretation. Schedules as has been designed are discussed as under :

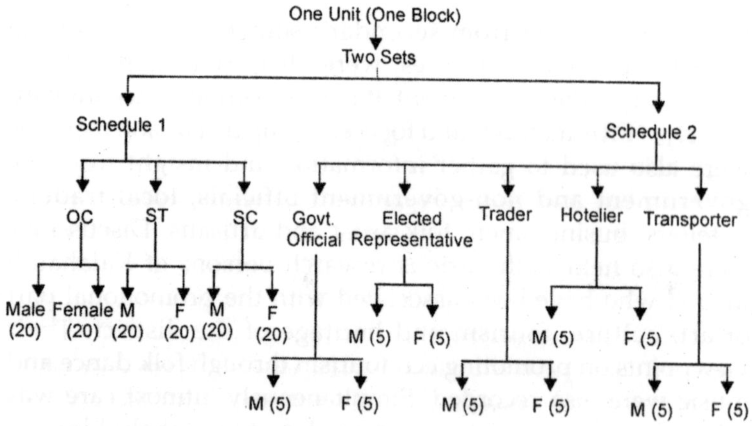

Fig. 1.1 : Design of Schedules

According to the above Fig. 1.1 in one unit Block a total number of 120 schedules have been administered among the folk artists. Although, the schedules were designed to canvas the equal number of female artists but due to non-availability of female practitioners, the study has considered the male counterparts. Likewise, a variation in the number of representatives of respective castes (OC, ST, SC) has been overlooked. The second schedule designed for the elite groups such as government officials, elected representatives, hoteliers, traders, transporters were administered among the targeted informants, 5 numbers each has been taken. On the whole, with utmost care the opinions of 1000 people have been taken into account for this research survey.

Data Processing and Analysis

Utmost care has been taken to process and analyse the data in a judicious manner. All the primary data have been duly processed and analysed by the computer device using the probable and projection method, statistical method and tabular analysis. The detailed analysis of the study has been discussed in the forthcoming chapters.

Research Limitations

The study was conducted in Kalahandi district in Orissa. This report has endeavoured to provide the authentic research information based on empirical data on folk dance and music of Kalahandi district. The research team has tried its best to project the report. The study was limited to folk artists, their art forms and the socio-economic problems. At the same time it has also tried to explore the tourism potentialities of the area with the motive of promoting eco-tourism in this backward region of Western Orissa under the light of the above-mentioned factors.

Chapterisation

The report has five chapters covering various dimensions of the present study. First chapter deals with the introduction and processes employed for the whole study. The second chapter provides basic information on folk artists and troupes of Kalahandi district. The third chapter covers folk artists and their socio-economic conditions. The fourth chapter explains the viability of eco-tourism in Kalahandi district. The fifth chapter provides a summary of the findings and policy recommendations of the study on the promotion of eco-tourism in the Western Orissa.

2

Folk Artists and Troupes of Kalahandi District

THE LAND AND THE PEOPLE

Folk as a common notion means a group of people who share a particular culture and identify themselves with a particular cultural area. Dundes (1965 : 2) has rightfully mentioned that the term folk can refer to any group of people whatsoever who share at least one common factor that could be a common occupation, language or religion but what is important is that a group formed for whatever reason will have some traditions of its own. We can say that a group must consist of many individuals who may not know each other but certainly are aware of the group traditions, which symbolizes the group core identity. According to Foster (1953 : 17), a folk culture characterizes a common way of life within a given area.

In Oriya literature meaning of Kalahandi is "black pot", which can be interpreted for its black cotton soil as evident from the black coloured earthen wheel pottery. It is also perceived as Jackpot of arts (*kalaa*) and culture.

Kalahandi : The Area

The district covers a geographical area of 7,920 sq.km that is approximately 5.09 per cent of the total geographical area of the State. There are 2 Sub-divisions, 7 Tahsils, 13 CD Blocks, 273 GPs and 6 Assembly Constituencies. The district headquarters is at Bhawanipatna (*District Statistical Handbook, Kalahandi—2001*). It has a total population of 13,35,494 out of which ST (61 types) and SC account for 28.65 per cent and 17.67 per cent respectively (Census, 2001). On account of the population, the Bhawanipatna Block constitutes the highest (2,01,192) and the Karlamunda Block (48,908) records the lowest in numbers (Census, 2001). The urban and rural population percentage are 7.50 per cent and 92.50 respectively. The literacy rate in the district is 45.94 per cent (*Economic Survey 2006-07*).

The district has magnificent scenic spots with beautiful hills and valleys. Standing on the hilltops one can see river valleys, shifting cultivation, forests etc. Kalahandi also boasts of pre-historic monuments, cave paintings, drawings at Gudahandi and Jogimathha near Khariar Block. Topographically, the region may be broadly divided into two distinct natural divisions—the hill tracts and the plain area. The mountains, hill tracts and streamlets of rivers surround the district. The hillsides are covered with dense Sal forest valleys and perennial streams.

Origin of Name

According to a popular belief, a mighty warrior of Rajputana came to this part and ruled it for many years. He named this part as 'Kalahambir' which in course of time changed into 'Kalahandi' (*Source* : Kalahandi District Gazette). According to the later interpretation, the name has possibly been derived from the pre-historic paintings of "Gudahandi" cave of Koksara Block. The name "Kalahandi" may literally justify as "black pot" or pot of arts. However, the interpretations regarding the origin of name of Kalahandi seems to be ambiguous. Junagarh was the headquarters of Kalahandi until 1849. For the first time the name "Kalahandi" was found in the Dadhibanar temple's inscription at Junagarh (now a district) which was the headquarters of the then Maharaja Jaya Shahi Deo. Later, the headquarters was shifted to Bhawanipatna (*Source* : Kalahandi District Gazetteer).

Folk Dance and Music

The folk song and dance of Kalahandi are a blend of fighter spirit, patriotism, spiritualism, love and romance, gracefulness etc. The regional dialect itself has its own identity and grace. Generally, the folk song is found to be influenced by the local regional dialect and accent. The way the songs and dances are identified one can conclude that they are packed and overflowing with energy. It is a general connotation that no one has ever composed nor deliberately attempted the tune and rhythm for the folk dance. Both the folk form of music and dance constitute the spontaneous endeavour of the folk mass of Kalahandi. People sing them to get pleasure, singing them amidst their sorrows and happiness, in their agony and ecstasy. Since time immemorial, the dance and the musical genre of the locality are found to be revered, cherished and cared by the people at large and has become synonymous with their sentiments.

Bhawanipatna Block

Bhawanipatna is named after the presiding deity Bhawanishankar Mahadev. In the topographical map of 1843, Bhawanipatna was known as Bhandeshwer and the presiding deity was Bhandeshwer Mahadev besides Manikeswari. In 1849, Maharaja Fatenarayan Deo shifted his headquarters from Junagarh (old fort) to Bhawanipatna and enshrined Bhawanishankar Mahadev and changed the name from Bhandeshwer to Bhawanipatna.

In the Block, seven folk troupes have been identified in three GPs, namely—Sadar (Five troupes), Medinipur (One troupe), Gadalipadar (one troupe), and are taken as the sample groups for this research study. Out of the seven troupes, five groups belong to *Ghumra* folk dance style although by different names such as (1) Bharati Ghumra Dala, (2) Jaya Maa Bhawaani Group, (3) Ghumra Karunda Kala Kendra, (4) Mahavir Sanskrutika Anushthana Ghumra Group, and (5) Shri Shri Balagopala Anushthana. These four groups have been taken from Sadar GP (Table 2.1). The rest troupes are—Shri Chaitanya Sankirtana Dala (Medinipur GP), and Thakurani Gananatya (Gadalipadar GP) who practice general folk dance and drama.

Ghumra

It is illustrated from Table 2.1 that Ghumra troupes are older in their formation state in comparison to the other dance groups of Bhawanipatna. The Bharati Ghumra Dala is the oldest troupe (more than 4 decades of formation) among all the groups (Photograph 2.1). The next two troupes, which came into existence are, namely Jaya Maa Bharati and Mahavir Sanskrutika Anushthana. Among them Karunda Kala Kendra Troupe is the youngest group (13 years).

Composition

The troupes are found to be unisexual (only male members) except Mahavir Sanskrutika Anushthana which constitutes both the male and female members in the ratio of 3 : 1 (Table 2.1). Generally, in a troupe the total membership accounts 18 to 20. It has been recorded that there are predominance of OBC members who belong to Gauda, Teli and Maali caste. The number of other performers such as ST, SC and general are at a very negligible rate (1-3 members).

Founded By

The troupes are formed by specially Ghumra experts who are known as 'Gurus'. It has been noticed that the respective Ghumra troupes (four) have different Gurus. They are Mr. Baishnav Rout, Mr. Dinabandhu Gahir, Mr. Madhu Majhi, Mr. Khirasindhu Raju and Mr. Jayanta Kumar Behera. It is learnt that under the initiation and motivation of these Gurus the members have joined the troupes. The Gurus irrespective of the caste, literal and social status have been respected and adored by the troupe members. The troupe members sincerely follow their preachings and instructions. Whenever and

Table 2.1 : Block-wise Distribution of Folk Artists in Kalahandi District

Sl. No.	Gram Panchayat	Name of group/Troupe	Year of Formation	Composition		Caste composition			
				Male/ Female/ Mixed	Total	ST	SC	OBC	GEN
		Bhawanipatna Block							
1.	Sadar GP	Bharati Ghumra Dal	1961	M	20	1	1	18	—
2.		Jaya Maa Bhawani Group	1991	M	18	2	1	15	—
3.		Ghumra Karunda Kala Kendra	1994	M	16	2	—	11	3
4.		Mahavir Sanskrutika Anushthan Ghumra group	1991	M-15F-05	20	—	4	13	3
5.		Sri Sri Balagopal Anushthana	1970	M	10	4	—	6	—
6.	Medinipur GP	Sri Chaitanya Sanskutika Dal	2005	M	10	2	—	6	2
7.	Gadalipadar GP	Thakurani Gananatya	2003	M	20	12	—	6	2
		Dharmagarh Block							
1.	Kharipadar GP	Sri Krishna Yuvak Sangha Prem Sankritana Dal	1972	M	12	3	4	5	—
2.		Khairipadar Nacha Party	1998	M	22	6	—	15	1
3.		Mere Sarabadha	1995	M	25	3	9	13	—
4.		Phulana Sundari Behrapara Natak Party	1996	M	20	4	6	10	—
5.	Chhilpa GP	Kuturu Baja Party	1998	M	12	—	12	—	—
6.		Duarsani Sanskrutika Kala Parishad	1992	M	20	3	—	17	—
7.		Ramaleela Geeti Natya	1994	M	20	—	5	15	—
8.		Maa Manikeswari Sanskrutika Anushthana	1997	M	10	—	—	10	—
9.		Maa Thakurani Bajasaala	1965	M	6	—	6	—	—

		Koksara Block						
1. Ampani GP	Kureiphul Group of Budha Raja Sanskrutika Anushthana, Ampani	1998	M-6 F-6	12	6	6	—	—
2.	Bajadala of Budha Raja Sanskrutika Anushthana	2001	M	10	6	—	4	—
3.	Maa Mangala Dal, Mandili	1990	M	11	11	—	—	—
4. Majhiguda GP	Jai Madhava Banabari Club	2004	M	14	—	8	6	—
5. Dudka Thenga GP	Khaligarh Pujhari Para Dal	2005	M	7	7	—	—	—
6.	Maa Thakuri Dal, Dandari Khaligarh	1990	M	9	7	2	—	—
7.	Kaligada Pujhari Para Dal	2005	M	7	7	—	—	—
		Lanjigarh Block						
1. Lanjigarh GP	Maa Bhairabi Kala Kendra Ghumra Dala	1972	M	20	—	—	20	—
2.	Agni Bhairabi Baja Party	1980	M	10	—	10	—	—
3.	Sankirtana Dal	1965	M	20	—	—	20	—
4.	Dhap Dance Party, Goipita	-do-	M	10	10	—	—	—
5. Chhatarpur GP	Dhap Dance Party, Bhataguda	-do-	F	10	10	—	—	—
6.	Dhap Dance Party, Leptaguda	1972	M	10	—	10	—	—
7. Trilochanpur GP	Dhap Dance Party, Khemundipadar	1975	M	05	5	—	—	—
8.	Adibasi Female Folk Dance, Ainthapadar	1950	F	10	10	—	—	—
9.	Adibasi Male Folk Dance, Kanakadu	1950	M	10	10	—	—	—
10.	Dhap Dance Party, Ladanga	Ancient	M	10	10	—	—	—
11.	Dhap Dance Party, Pheldanek	-dc-	M	10	10	—	—	—
		Narla Block						
1. Narla GP	Sri Ram Navami Committee	1980	M	10	2	—	7	1
2. Rupra Road GP	Dharani Dhar Ghumra Committee	1977	M	10	10	—	—	—

Sl. No.	Gram Panchayat	Name of group/Troupe	Year of Formation	Composition		Caste composition			
				Male/ Female/ Mixed	Total	ST	SC	OBC	GEN
3.		Majhali Para Ghumra Party	1967	M	11	11	—	—	—
4.	Tulapada GP	Birat Parva Party, Badapada	1975	M	20	15	—	4	1
5.	Mandel GP	Ram Leela Troupe, Ashuragarh	1976	M	20	—	—	20	—
6.		Jaga Balia Sankirtan Madala	2000	M	15	2	1	12	—
7.	Sargiguda GP	Maa Majhigauri Natak Committee	2000	M	20	9	—	11	—
8.	Kandel GP	Sri Sri Singhababini Jagadhatri Gana Natya	1965	M	10	2	—	8	—
		Thuamul Rampur Block							
1.	Th. Rampur GP	Maa Manikeswari Dal	1997	M	12	1	1	10	—
2.	Gunupur GP	Salap Nishan	Ancient	M	10	2	5	3	—
3.		Lankeswari Ghumra Party	1974	M	12	—	—	12	—
4.		Maa Thakurani Sanskrutika Kala Parishad	2005	M	12	6	6	—	—
5.		Khandarla Nacha Party	2005	M	8	5	3	—	—
6.		Brundabati Dal	1930	M-6F-6	12	10	2	—	—
7.		Maa Thakurani Dal, Harijan Pada	2000	M	6	—	6	—	—
8.		Madingaraja Dhap Party	Ancient	M-10F-10	20	20	—	—	—
9.	Kanigumma GP	Kanigumma Ghumra Dal	2003	M	12	—	4	8	—
8.	Gopalpur GP	Dhap Dance Party, Sargiguda	Ancient	M-5F-5	10	6	2	2	—

wherever in case of any conflict between the members, it is solved in an amicable way by the coordination of the Gurus.

Objectives

The objectives of the troupes are as follows :

- To entertain the people and spectators.
- To make people aware about the folk dance and cultural heritage of Kalahandi.
- To preserve the folk culture and tradition of Kalahandi.
- To reveal the dynamism of marital arts through the arts.
- To spread awareness about the cohesiveness of community/group.
- To enhance economic status of the group.
- To strengthen the group as well as to bring laurels for the group.
- To keep up the traditional values of Ghumra dance.
- To inculcate good qualities such as self-discipline, group discipline, faithfulness and obedience to the Guru of the group.
- To keep up the prestige of own locality/*pada*.
- To build the group as a good group.
- To transform the group into best Ghumra troupe.

Training

Generally, they get training from their respective Guru for a period of four months to one year depending on one's personal learning ability. Training place is generally located at the village altar (*mandap*), under a banyan tree or at the youth club house (Photograph 2.2). They do not have to pay for their training. It is the voluntary contribution of the respective Guru to the respective troupe. The practice timing is generally limited to three to four hours daily. The objectives of the training are :

- To upgrade the dance style and form.

- To keep in touch with the folk dance and rhythmic style.
- To be in touch with the Guru and his skills.
- To rectify one's own mistakes.
- To learn more about the instruments.
- To gain expertise in the dance and acquire the skill of coordination between dance and music.
- To learn the skills and techniques of the Ghumra dance.
- To participate in the State and district level competitions and win the prize.
- To earn laurels for the group.
- To transform the troupe into the best Ghumra troupe.
- To obey to the Guru in order to maintain unity and integrity within the group.

Structural Composition of the Group

In the group there are ten to twenty members who have defined roles to play which is described (Figure 2.1) as below.

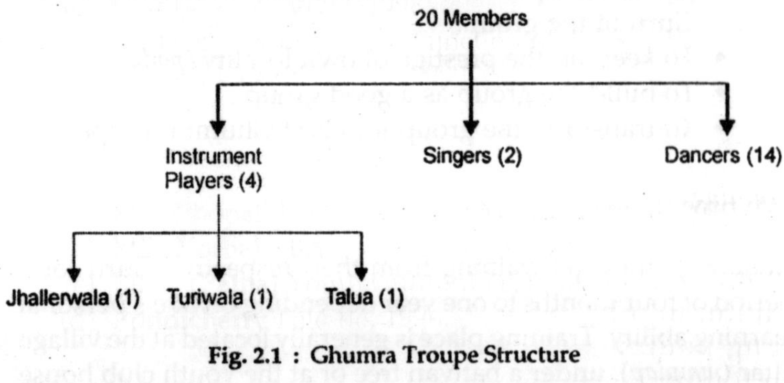

Fig. 2.1 : Ghumra Troupe Structure

Generally, the instrument players are known after the name of the respective instruments they play such as Jhallerwala, Turiwala and Talua. Dancers are known as *Nachaniya*.

Ghumra and its Origin

Legendry tradition says that the term 'Ghumra' has been derived from the word *ghum* or *ghumuri* which means an earthen pot (Photograph 2.3). It is also said that while playing, the instrument sounds like *ghum* that is why it is named as 'Ghumra'. The instrument is a two feet hollow earthen pot, which looks like a long pitcher with a cover of *iguana* skin. The body of the instrument is cylindrical in shape and the face of the instrument is V-shaped. During dancing, the instrument is tied on the waist and left shoulder of the dancer. Interestingly, its counterpart known as Ghumri, a round shaped earthen pot, which is used by the young girls of Kalahandi to fetch water from the ponds and the rivers. According to Dr. Mahendra Kumar Mishra (2002 : 2-3), historically it dates back to 1000 years ago as the 'Natamandapa of Konark Temple' depicts the images of male Ghumra dance which indicates the practice of Ghumra dance during the rule of Ganga kings of Orissa. Even the dance form has a mythological connection as the epics of *Mahabharata, Chandipurana, Ramayana* and many other *Puranas* reveal the practice of Ghumra.

The sounds created from the musical instruments have a phonemic impact on both the body and the mind. In the ancient time, the Ghumra was used in the battle fields to invoke the fighting spirit in the warriors against the opponents. It used to be performed both during the war time and also during the peace time to entertain the common people.

During pre-independence era (1930), the Ghumra was a Darbari dance of Kalahandi Raja. Subsequently, the dance continued to be performed both in folk and Darbari traditions. During the early post-independence period, Mr. P.K. Deo, the then Maharaja of Kalahandi patronized this dance form as the State dance of Kalahandi.

Modern Attribute

In the present era, Ghumra is considered to be war drum of demon Gosima Asur as well as the war dance of Goddess

Durga. It is believed that Goddess Durga never possesses in a shaman unless she is charged with the majestic drumming sound of Ghumra. Since time immemorial, this dance has been a part of the ritual performance in the temples of Goddess Manikeshwari, Goddess Lankeshwari, Goddess Samaleshwari, Goddess Dwaarasani and Goddess Bastaaren. During Dusehra festival, the Ghumra troupe lead the *Chattar* (the symbolic representation of Goddess Manikeshwari) procession at Bhawanipatna (Photographs 2.4 and 2.5). Another Oriya festival called as 'Kumara Purnima', the Ghumra dance competitions are organized throughout the district. A panel of judges evaluates the dance from the angle of costumes, music, rhythmic composition of songs, dance gestures and style etc. For the competition, the Ghumra parties go on a procession towards the venue. At times, the dancers even visit from house to house in order to earn some money for their troupe's activities.

Competitions

When the competition is held between two groups, the audiences generally support the group they like and they also encourage that group. During competitions, the questions based on the Hindu mythology are asked. A singer from one troupe asks the questions and the opposite group answers it spontaneously. If the group is not able to answer then it is declared as defeated troupe. Interestingly, the winner troupe starts teasing the loser troupe with humorous jokes and songs. Thus, each competition is adjudged as a platform through which the troupes try to acquire better performance skills.

Theme of the Song

The theme of the song is found to be changed according to the time, situation and surrounding. It has been recorded that songs are composed as according to the suitability of the occasion. During welcome of VIP, Ministers, mass awareness programmes and community mobilization programmes, the themes are modified suitably. Modern folk songs, namely Sambalpuri and Oriya pop music are also used for the dance performance to attract the spectators. The electronic media such as the radio and the television and the paper have disseminated the folk form of Ghumra dance. Accordingly, there has been a great impact of modernity in the attire, costumes and themes of the songs.

Dance Style

The team consists of even number of artists. The Ghumra artists arrange themselves in circular, semi-circular, triangular and two or three straight lines. They dance on the rhythm of the instruments (Photograph 2.1).

Musical Instruments

The Ghumra dance generally is associated with six type of instruments (Photograph 2.6) which are Jhallar, Nisan, Turi and Tal, Ghumra and Chemta (Table 2.3). Generally, the instruments are traditional and are purchased from Junagarh of Kalahandi district, Raipur of Madhya Pradesh and other places of Orissa. Among all the instruments, Nisan and Turi are the costlier ones. An instrument is played for eight months as the Ghumra dance is commonly performed for eight months in a year. The instrument players only possess their respective instruments. The dancers do not possess any instrument.

- Ghumra—It is made up of *Iguana's* skin. It is a traditional instrument. It costs about Rs. 500 to Rs. 1,000.
- Nisan—It is made of cast iron and is covered by cattle's skin. It costs about Rs. 1,700 to Rs. 2,000 each.
- Chemta—The body of this instrument is made of brass and the face is covered with cattle's skin. It is again a traditional instrument and costs about Rs. 400.
- Turi—It is a wind instrument made of brass which costs about Rs. 1,200 and is bought from Bhubana of Dhenkanal district.

- Tal—It is made of brass and silver, which makes sound when it shakes. The modern form of this instrument costs about Rs. 200 to Rs. 500 and is bought from Cuttack, Khariar and Junagarh.
- Jhaller—It is made up of Peacock's feathers and is traditional by nature. It is bought from Rajasthan and costs about Rs. 1,000 to Rs. 2,000.

Costumes and Jewellery

The costume includes their traditional dress and ornaments, which they use during their performance. They use a typical style of attire—head gear (*pagdi*), armlets (*tahia* and *bahuti*), large ear rings (*kundala*), necklace (*galaamaali*), colourful pyjama, shirt, pants and *dhoti* (Photograph 2.1). It has been recorded that their dress attire is more costly than their ornaments (Table 2.2). It is illustrated from the table that on an average, a troupe member possesses the costumes costing around Rs. 1,600 to Rs. 2,000.

Social Relations

Although, the Ghumra legend says that the dance is a pure tribal dance but in course of time the non-tribal people such as SC, OBC and General caste people have started learning the art of Ghumra. In the village the troupe members observe social restrictions with the SC people but in the troupe, they do not observe any restriction.

At the village level, they observe all types of socio-cultural restrictions of life cycle rituals. On the other hand, except in cases of death rituals, the troupe members do not observe any socio-cultural restrictions at the troupe levels. In case of observance of funeral rituals they observe ten to twelve days of restrictions till the over of communal feast on the 12th day.

Conflicts

There are cases of family conflicts, which arise due to excess liquor consumption, late night reporting to homes etc. But these

Table 2.2 : Costumes and Jewellery used by Troupes in Kalahandi District

Sl. No.	*Name of the Costume/ jewellery*	*Purchased from*	*Cost (in Rs.)*
1.	Pagadi	Junagarh	150
2.	Tahia	-do-	200
3.	Bahuti	-do-	20
4.	Ghunghuru	-do-	50
5.	Kundala	-do-	25
6.	Galamaali	Bh. Patna, Raipur	20
7.	Colourful Shirt	-do-	500
8.	Pant	-do-	500
9.	AntaPatti	-do-	50
10.	Galapatti	-do-	30
11.	Dhoti	-do-	50
12.	Gamchha	-do-	30
13.	Vest	-do-	20
14.	Clip	Junagarh, Raipur	5-10
15.	Khagla	Junagarh	20
16.	Ghika	-do-	50
17.	Katriya	-do-	50
18.	Saanju (chest guard)	-do-	50-100
19.	Bala (bangle)	-do-	10-100
20.	Bala (iron bracelet)	Junagarh, Bh. Patna	20-50
21.	Kada (bangle)	-do-	20-50
22.	Bandira	Junagarh	20-40
23.	Painri (anklet)	-do-	20-30
24.	Coloured beaded necklace	-do-	10-20
25.	Kendu stick	—	—
26.	Blackberry branches	—	—
27.	Sleeveless coats	Junagarh, Bh.Patna	200
28.	Rudraksh	-do-	200-2000
29.	Vermillion	-do-	5-10
30.	Tabji (armlet)	-do-	200-500
31.	Tulsi maali (necklace made out of Tulsi)	—	—
32.	Chandan maali (necklace made out of sandalwood)	Bh.Patna	20-30
33.	Sandalwood beads	-do-	10-30
34.	Coloured paper	-do-	10
35.	Coloured cloths	-do-	50-100
36.	Artificial sword	Bh. Patna, Junagarh	20-50
37.	Artificial Bow and Arrow	-do-	20-50
38.	Wrist watch	Bh. Patna	100-2000
39.	Imitations	-do-	5-50
40.	Colourful Saari	-do-	100-200
41.	Blouse	-do-	30-50
42.	Perfume	-do-	10-20
43.	Powder	-do-	10-30
44.	Tihaya	-do-	10-30
45.	Kajal	-do-	5-10

problems are solved with the intervention of elderly persons. Troupe conflicts occur when there is lack of coordination among fellow troupe members. Also, sometimes it happens due to mismanagement of the troupe's administration. However, the respective Guru of the troupe solves such conflicts.

Participation in Cultural Events

It has been recorded that the Ghumra parties have been participating in various cultural festivals at the Block, panchayat, district, state and national levels (Table 2.4). It is depicted from the tables that Mahavir Sanskrutika Anushthana is the only troupe to take part in the national level competitions at Delhi trade fair during 2006 under the sponsorship of Information and Public Relations Department, Government of Orissa. However, the artist, except availing opportunity of visiting Delhi has not received any other benefits. It has been seen evidently from the tables that more often the same troupe attends the competitions for years as other do not get a chance. One such example may be of Mahavir Sanskrutika Anushthana Ghumra troupe which has attended National Youth Festival four times now (2001-04) organized at the State level of Andhra Pradesh, Pondicherry and Kerala under the sponsorship of Ministry of Youths and Sports. For this trip, the troupe has availed the economic benefit of Rs. 5,000. The troupe Jaya Maa Bhawani Ghumra Dal has visited the State capital Bhubaneswar to attend a television programme of National Oriya channel in 1999 under the sponsorship of District Cultural Council. Except availing travel allowance of Rs. 500, the troupe has not gained any economic benefit. The tables state that all the troupes have been performing at the village level during various auspicious religious celebrations such as Dusehra, Laxmi Puja, Nua Khai and Jhamujatra with the help of village committee. For these trips, except free flooding they do not avail any other benefits. Likewise, they have also participated in Panchayat level and Block level (Photograph 2.1). It has been revealed that during the Block level competitions Jaya Maa Bhawani and Karunda

Kala Kendra have earned the laurels from the Block committee. Bharati Ghumra troupe is yet to get any opportunity to perform outside their Block unlike other Ghumra troupes of Bhawanipatna. Shri Shri Balagopal Anushthana Ghumra troupe is the only troupe to attend boat rowing celebration (Boita-bandhaana celebration) at Paradip port of Kendrapada district under the sponsorship of Ministry of Cultural Affairs.

Shri Chaitanya Sankirtana Dala

The troupe comprises ten male members. The Medinipur village committee (Medinipur GP) of under self-motivation formed the group in the year 2005. The members belong to two nearby villages of Medinipur GP. The caste composition of the group is—2 (ST), 6 (OBC) and 2 (General). The objectives of the troupe are :

- To invoke Lord Vishnu through prayers/*sankirtana* (clapping hands);
- To aspire for supernatural blessings and salvation;
- To make people aware of God's omnipresence; and
- To establish feeling of obeisance and devotion through prayers and *sankirtana.*

Training

The members have undergone training for six months at the village level by Guru Saroj Sathpathy at free of cost. The purposes behind the training are :

- To play instrument (*khuli khanjani*) correctly in accordance with another instrument *Khola.*
- To become a good devotional singer.

Daily, the group devotes at least two hours in singing *sankirtanas* for better performance at the centre place of the village.

Theme

The theme is based on devotional prayers of Krishna and Radha. Apart from that, the song is composed to invoke the God for welfare of the humanity and human beings.

Musical Instrument

They possess two traditional instruments—Khola and Ginni (small cymbal). The Khola/Khanjani is made of mud, a cotton string, cattle skin and Babul wood. But traditionally it used to be made of Iguana skin. These days due to lesser Iguana population cattle skin is preferred. It costs about Rs. 250 to Rs. 300. It is purchased from Junagarh Block of Kalahandi district and Nabarangpur Block of Koraput district. Ginni is a pair of an alloy of brass and copper plates and costs about Rs. 200 to Rs. 300. This instrument is purchased from Junagarh of Kalahandi district. Both the instruments are played during Kartika Purnima in the months of November and December.

Costumes and Jewellery

They do not use any particular costumes or jewellery. Normally, they clad themselves in simple attire, which includes a *dhoti,* a piece of cloth (*gamchha*) on the shoulder and a vest. These are made of cotton and costs about Rs. 300 in total.

Social Relationship

They only welcome ST (Kandha and Sabara) and OBC (Maali and Gouda) newcomers to their 'Sankirtana' party. They do not accept food, water, beverage, smoking and marriage proposals from SC (washerman, barber and damba people). Even, they do not allow these people to touch them and enter into their houses. But for their agricultural work, the SC people are permitted. It has been recorded that they observe socio-cultural restrictions during the birth of a newborn child and death rituals at the family, village and troupe levels.

Participation

It is found that (Table 2.4) their performance of *Sankirtana* is only limited to nearby villages, namely—Jaganathpur, Ichhapur and Medinipur villages and Gram Panchayats namely Lanjigarh, Danguagarh and Gudlipadar. Every year during Kartika Purnima (November and December) they roam around the surrounding villages and localities early in the morning and in the evening time.

Thakurani Gananatya

Mr. Sarojkant Satpathy who is the Director and Writer of this folk drama formed the group comprising twenty male members in 2003. He belongs to the same locality. Under his motivation, the members have voluntarily joined this dance troupe. The group consists of more number of ST (12) members, OBC (2) members and only General (2) members (Table 2.1). The founder person Mr. Saroj Satpathy is called as 'Master of the Troupe' and he gives training to the trainees at least for two to three months without any charge. The trainees and the permanent troupe members do practice at their village club house 'Kedara Udita Yuvak Sangha' at Ichhapur village. It has been recorded that members regularly attend the troupe activities.

Troupe's Objective

- To bring laurels to the troupe.
- To maintain communal harmony and unity among the villagers and the youth.
- To make people aware of their civic duties, social and communal rights and privileges.

Theme

Since this is a folk drama troupe, so there are folk songs, music, dance and dialogues. The subject matter of the folk drama keeps on changing and accordingly the theme also changes. As a general practice, the theme is based on Indian epics and mythology, namely—*Mahabharata, Ramayana, Mahisasura Vadha* etc. They also give performances on mass awareness programmes, namely—Malaria and AIDS eradication, Pulse Polio and Literacy Campaigns. They do not use any instruments. They express their feelings through action and singing performance.

Costumes and Jewellery

They use trousers, shirts, socks and shoes as per the requirement of the drama characters at the time of performance. A member of the troupe uses the costumes that costs about Rs. 100 to Rs. 300 (Table 2.2). The troupe uses various types of jewellery such as—Bangles (*bala*), Big Earings (*kundala*), a chest guard (*saanju*), a head gear, neck band (*galapatti*), arm plate (*bahuti*) and zinc which in total costs about Rs. 585 (Table 2.2).

Conflicts

The reason behind the conflicts is mainly excess liquor consumption habits that lead to disputes in the family as well as the troupe. Sometimes, in the troupe the conflict arises due to lack of proper understanding and coordination. The family conflict is solved by the father of the household and troupe master in the troupe level.

Social Relationship

It has been noted from their interviews that except SC people, all other people are accepted by the troupe. Similarly, they also obey the socio-cultural restrictions with these people. Regarding the socio-cultural restrictions, in case of life cycle rituals, they obey these at the family level but in the troupe level except in case of death rituals they do not follow any restrictions.

Participation of Troupes in Cultural Events

Except Block, Panchayat and village levels, the troupe has not so far given any performance anywhere outside. It has been depicted in Table 2.4 that during their participation in 2000 at village, Panchayat and Block levels, the troupe received financial support of Rs. 5,500. During this trip although, they have faced various problems such as improper light arrangements, lack of electricity, and travel allowances, still they have enjoyed their trips. It is also learnt that the visit to Vedanta Aluminium Ltd. (2005) in Lanjigarh Block was most enjoyable and comfortable for the troupe members.

Expectations

It has been recorded that the artists have to face financial problems. They have also stated that they are deprived of proper opportunities unlike other districts. When enquired about their expectations, they said that they should be provided with modern musical instruments and a club house for their promotion of dance activities. At the same time, they optimistically have mentioned the positive motive of their folk form of dance.

Dharmagarh Block

Dharmagarh is situated at 45 km away from the district headquarters. In this Block nine troupes have been identified in two GPs, namely—Khairipadar and Chhilpa (Table 2.1). It has been recorded that each party has its own core identity. Out of the nine groups, two are Ghumra parties, namely—Maa Manikeshwari Sanskrutika Anushthana and Maa Thakurani Bajasaala. Maa Thakurani Bajasaala is the oldest in its formation (42 years). The others are Shri Krishna Yuvak Sangha Prem Sankirtana Dal, Khairipadar Nacha Party, Mera Sarabadha, Khulana Sundari Beherapada Nacha Party, Kuturu Baja Party, Duarasaani Sanskrutika Kala Parishad and Rama Leela Geeti Natya.

Ghumra Troupes

The Ghumra troupes composed of male members and the membership is limited to six to ten members. Maa Manikeshwari Sanskrutika Anushthana (year of formation is 1997) is younger than Maa Thakurani Bajasaala and is composed of ten OBC members (Table 2.1). Whereas, Maa Thakurani Bajasaala is the oldest and only possesses six ST (Kandha) members. The founder member of both the parties are different. Gujjar Kumar founded Maa Thakurani Bajasaala. Paneshwar Panigrahi formed Maa Manikeshwari Sanskrutika Anushthana. Both the founders belonged to the same locality. The members voluntarily have joined the troupes. The members of Maa Thakurani Bajasaala do not attend the troupe activities regularly because this group gives the performance only during the marriage functions of fellow villagers. These troupe's sole objective is to earn money from the performances. The members have not undergone any formal training. They practice only out of their hobbies. There is no certain folk song of this party as their performance is only restricted to the marriage processions. So, they perform according to the contemporary traditions. During the time of performance, they put on formal dress which costs about Rs. 200 to Rs. 500. Maa Manikeshwari Sanskrutika Anushthana on the other hand has a strict code of conduct for its troupe members. The members meet daily at the central place of the village to practice (Photograph 2.7).

Musical Instruments

The musical instruments used by these troupes are Nisan, Chanta, Dhola, Mrudunga, Ginni, Casio, Jhumka, Tassa, Mahuri and cycle spokes. Nisan is a traditional instrument and shaped like a cylindrical drum, which is covered by a thin cattle skin membrane and costs about Rs. 1,000. The Chanta is also a traditional instrument and costs about Rs. 20. Among all the instruments, Casio and Jhumkas are modern instruments (Photograph 2.8).

Maintenance

The maintenance of the instrument is done by the troupe's contribution. In case of requirement of a new instrument, the members contribute and purchase the instrument.

Social Relationship

In the village, they obey the social restrictions. While in the troupe, all the members irrespective of caste and tribe are welcome. There is no restriction in exchange of gifts, agricultural works, touch and even entering into houses.

Participation of Troupes in Cultural Events

Maa Manikeshwari Sanskrutika troupe has been taking part in cultural festivals in other State, namely, Chhattisgarh during Dusehra occasion every year under the sponsorship of District Cultural Committee. It has also participated in Block level Kalahandi Mahotsava (Photograph 2.9). For this performance they have gained the additional income of Rs. 2,000 to Rs. 3,000. It is learnt from the table that Maa Thakurani Bajasaala, the other troupe has only participated in Block level Cultural events.

Financial Assistance

It has been recorded that except from fellow artists and family members, they do not get any financial assistance from other government officials, NGOs or others.

Expectation

It is learnt that they need financial support and a new story lines for the promotion of their dance activities.

Other Seven Troupes

The seven troupes are composed of male members. Shri Krishna Yuvak Sangha Prema Sankirtana Dal and Kuturu Baja Party have twelve members each in their troupes. Mere Sarbadha Party is represented by twenty-five members. The Khairipadar Nacha Party has twenty-two members. The rest three troupes, namely—Khulana Sundari Beherapara Natak Party, Duarasaani Sanskrutika Kala Parishad and Ramaleela Geet Natya have twenty members in each troupe. Kuturu Baja Party (Photograph 2.10) and Ramaleela Geet Natya do not have any ST members. Khairipadar Nacha Party and Duarasaani Sanskrutika Kala Parishad do not have any SC members. Except for Khairipadar Nacha Party, none of the troupes possess any membership from the General Category. Among the seven troupes, Shri Krishna Yuvak Sangha Prema Sankirtana Dal is the oldest troupe (25 years) whereas, the other troupes are more or less only one decade old.

Theme

The theme of each of the troupe varies from the other. Generally, the theme is based on the objective of the respective troupe. For example, the objective of Shri Krishna Yuvak Sangha Prema Sankirtana Dal, Duarasaani Sansrutika Kala Parishad and Mere Sarbadha is to create the spiritual motives among the people. Accordingly, the folk song is based on the devotional feeling. On the other hand, the objective of Khairipadar Nacha Party, Phulana Sundari Nacha Party and Ramaleela Geet Natya is to entertain the guest by composing dance drama which is based on epics such as the *Mahabharata, Ramayana,* etc. Kuturu Baja Party is the only party, which performs during the marriage ceremonies and consists only of six SC members. This troupe does not follow any single theme but keeps on following different themes depending upon the contemporary music.

Jewellery and Costumes

The troupes, which perform for devotional themes use traditional attire like *dhoti, gamchha* and vests. Besides, they apply sandalwood paste on their foreheads, wrists and arms. The common jewellery they use are beads of sandalwood, rudraksh, armlet (*tabji*), iron bracelet (*bala*), sandalwood necklace (*chandan maali*), tulsi necklace (*tulasi maali*), which in total costs about Rs. 350 to Rs. 550. The folk drama groups, which perform on mythological themes dress themselves in modern as well as traditional attire. The jewellery also varies according to the attire. They use various types of beads, coloured paper, coloured clothes, artificial sword, bow and arrow, etc. Such costumes cost them about Rs. 1,500 to Rs. 2,000.

Musical Instrument

The devotional troupes play instruments like Kebji, a traditional brass instrument that costs about Rs.100. It is mostly played in Kartika Purnima during the months of November and December. Another traditional instrument called as Khola, made of mud and cattle skin, costs about Rs. 1,500 to Rs. 2,000. Besides, instruments like Gini and Khanjani are also used for the devotional songs. The dance drama troupes play Dholla (double membraned drum), Mrudunga (cylindrical drum), Gini (small cymbal), Jhumka and Casio which in total costs about Rs. 4,500 to Rs. 4,700 (Table 2.3).

Maintenance

The maintenance of the instruments is done with the help of the contributions given by the troupe members. If there is any necessity of any new instrument, the members contribute and the money is utilized.

Social Relationship

During the life cycle rituals, the artists obey and follow all the socio-cultural rules and restrictions at the individual levels. But in the troupe, such restrictions are not obeyed.

Table 2.3 : Musical Instruments of Folk Troupes in Kalahandi District

Name	*Cost*	*Made by*	*Place of Purchase*	*Type of instrument*	
				Traditional	*Modern*
Jhaller	400-600	Others	Junagarh	Yes	No
Nisan	1200-1500	Others	Junagarh, B. Patana	Yes	No
Turi	1000-1200	Others	Bhubana	Yes	Yes
Tall	200-1200	Others	Cuttack	Yes	No
Tali	500-600	Others	Khariar, Junagarh	Yes	No
Kohali	900-1000	Others	Junagarh	Yes	No
Jhaller	100-400	Others	Junagarh	Yes	No
Ghumra	1000-1200	Others	Junagarh	Yes	No
Nisan	200-500	Others	B. Patna	Yes	No
Chanta	20	Others	B. Patna	Yes	No
Ram Tali	20	Self	—		
Dhap	200-300	Other	Junagarh, Rayagada	Yes	No
Talua	30-40	Self	—		
Salap Nishan	1000-2000	Other	Junagarh	Yes	No
Chemta	200-500	Other	Junagarh	Yes	No
Ginni	200	Other	Junagarh	Yes	No
Dhol	500-700	Other	Bhawani-patna, Junagarh, Raipur	Yes	No
Mridunga	1000-2000	Other	Raipur, Junagarh, N. Pur	Yes	No
Casio	2000-4000	Other	Chatisgarh (MP), Cuttack	No	Yes
Jhumka	500-700	Other	Raipur, Junagarh and B.Patna	No	Yes
Tassa	400-500	Other		Yes	No
Mahuri	700-800	Other	Raipur, Junagarh	Yes	Yes
Kebji	200	Other	Cuttack, Dhenkanala, Junagarh	Yes	No
Khola	1500 to 2000	Other	Junagarh, Cuttack, Raipur	Yes	Yes

Table 2.3—contd.

Name	Cost	Made by	Place of Purchase	Type of instrument	
				Traditional	Modern
Maadala	500	Other	Junagarh	Yes	No
Mundari Baja	3000	Other	Junagarh	Yes	No
Taal	200	Other	Junagarh	Yes	No
Doodra	20	Self	—	Yes	No
Tidibidi	30	Self	—	Yes	No
Timtin	50	Self	—	Yes	No
Sedrum	50-100	Self	—	Yes	No
Ram Taali	60-100	Self/Other	—	Yes	No
Dolina	60-100	Self/Other	—	Yes	No
Jhanja	70-200	Other	Junagarh	Yes	No
Singh Baja	1000-2000	Other	Junagarh	Yes	No
Sankha	20-50	—	Junagarh	Yes	No
Tasha wallah	20-200	Other	Junagarh	Yes	No
Cycle spokes	10-50	Self/Other	Own place	No	Yes
Total-38 types Instruments	(200-2000) Troupe/s possession	Self/Other	(Junagarh) Majority	(Yes) Majority	(No) Majority

Conflict

At the troupe level, the conflicts arise mostly due to irregular attendance as well as personal rivalry. The Guru of the respective troupe settles such disputes.

Participation in the Cultural Events

The devotional troupes performances are limited within the districts. Every year, during the festival of Kartika Purnima in the months of November and December, the troupe goes on a procession within the village, Gram Panchayat and the district, chanting devotional songs in the name of Lord Vishnu and Chaitanya Mahaprabhu. In the year 2001 and 2003, these troupes have participated in the Block level and district level *utsav* organized by the Block and District cultural councils. For the trip, they have not availed any TA/DA. The dance drama troupes have attended village level, Panchayat level and Block level cultural events and various occasions such as Durga Puja, Dusehra, personal affairs such as marriages and reportedly they received Rs. 3,000 to Rs. 4,000 for each of their performances.

Financial Assistance

Both the dance drama troupes and the devotional troupes manage to get the financial support for the sustenance of their troupe activities from fellow artists as well as the family members.

Expectations

The members of the devotional troupe claim to need new musical instruments, a place for practice and financial aid to promote their *Sankirtana* activities. The folk dramatists hope for modern musical instruments, new storylines, financial help, good road infrastructure, electricity and a place for their practice.

Koksara Block

The Koksara Block is located at a distance of 61 km from the district headquarters. A total number of seven folk dance troupes have been identified in three Gram Panchayats and taken as the study troupes (Table 2.1). Each troupe has its own identity. The folk troupe Kureiphula is the only mixed troupe that constitutes both the male and female members in equal composition (male-6, female-6). The group is one decade old (year of formation—1998) and has both SC (Damba) and ST (Batahada, Kandha) members. The troupes, namely Maa Mangala Dal (Photograph 2.11) and Maa Thakurani Dal are the oldest troupes (existing since last two decades). Maa Mangala Dal is the only troupe, which possesses all ST members. Maa Thakurani Dal has a total of nine members out of which seven belong to ST (Damba) and two to SC (Bhatra). The Baaja Dal constitutes six ST (Kandha) and four OBC

(Gauda) male members. Jaya Madhab Banabaari Club (Photograph 2.12) is four years old and has 14 members out of which eight belong to SC and six belong to OBC. Khaligarh Pujari Pada Dal and Kaligada Pujari Pada Dal each consist of seven male members and this is a pure ST group (Parajaa and Kandha). It is comparatively a younger group (year of formation—2005). Each troupe has its own core essence of folk identity, which is described as below :

Aampani Gram Panchayat

The troupes in Aampani GP are Kureiphula Troupe :

1. Kureiphula group of Budhaaraja Sanskrutika Anushthana (Photograph 2.13).
2. Baaja Dal of Budhaaraja Sanskrutika Anushthana (Photograph 2.14).
3. Maa Mangala Dal (Photograph 2.11).

The founder members of Kureiphula Group are Ruturaj Majhi and Bijay Kumar Naik. Ruturaj Majhi is also the founder of Baaja Dal. Their dance, being a seasonal dance, is only performed during the Car Festival (*Ratha Jaatra*). They perform on the first day of the festival and retreat on the very next day followed by a local festival called as Nua Khai. Since the period of performance is limited, the members tend to be irregular in attending their troupe activities. While, Maa Mangla Dal troupe has been continuing to perform for generations. The members of this group do not undergo any training as this is their inherited skill.

The objectives of these troupes are :

- To preserve folk songs and folk tradition.
- To earn laurels for the troupe.
- To inculcate good qualities such as skill of coordination, sincerity, obedience, humbleness, sublimity, etc.
- To worship mother earth, Maa Manikeshwari and village deity for good cultivation and communal harmony.

Theme

The Kureiphula troupe is named after a wild flower called as 'kuraiphula'. It is well known for its beauty and fragrance but the flower withers away unnoticeably. The folk dance is considered to be as charming, beautiful and adorable as the wild flower by the villagers. The content is dual type—(a) invoke and worship village deity for the welfare of the village; and (b) description of the scenic beauty of the mother nature. While, the contents of the folk song Baaja Dal depicts that in the ancient time there was no proper road to their village. So the people used to use a big teak log to cross the muddy village road. During the performance, the dancers move holding blackberry branches or only a piece of branch in their hands as if they were holding the teak logs. The dance moves are synchronized with the rhythmic drum beatings and sounds of double membraned drum (*madala*). The folk song of Maa Mangala Dal is based on worship of Maa Manikeshwari.

Costumes and Jewellery

All the troupes dress themselves in mostly modern attire which more or less constitutes the following items—*dhoti*, shirt, vest, *gamchha*, neck tie (*gala pati*), arm let (*baahuti*), big earrings (*kundala*), coloured beaded necklace, wrist watch, rings, *kajal*, zinc, vermilion and headgear which in total costs about Rs. 500 to Rs. 600. It is depicted from Table 2.2 that the female members of Kureiphula group use different colourful *saries*, blouses, fancy imitation jewelleries, bangles, powder, vermilion, perfumes etc. that cost about Rs. 200 to Rs. 500. Besides these, the Baaja *dal* members hold blackberry branches during their performance.

Musical Instruments

The Kureiphula troupe does not possess any musical instruments because they sing and dance simultaneously. Baaja *dal* plays a cylindrical double faced drum (*madal*) which is made of *babul* wood, tree rope (*kaincha* tree) and cattle skin membrane and costs about Rs. 500 (Table 2.3). Another instrument used by this group, named as *Mundari baja,* is made of iron and costs about Rs. 3,000. Maa Mangala Dal also uses *jhumka* and *taal* besides the other instruments which costs about Rs. 150 to Rs. 200 (Table 2.3). The troupe also uses Doodra, a traditional instrument, which is made of tree branch and bamboo sticks and costs about Rs. 20 each. The maintenance of the musical instruments is taken care of by the contributions made to the troupes by its respective members.

Socio-cultural Restrictions

All the three troupes are welcoming by nature to people from other communities at the village level. However, they abide by social restrictions at the individual level when it comes down to SC (Damba) people. The areas of restriction are food, water, beverage, smoke, rituals, touch, entering into the houses and agricultural work.

Conflicts

It has been recorded that conflicts in these groups have occurred because of misunderstanding, lack of coordination between the members, mismanagement of money earned etc. However, these conflicts are found to be solved by the respective group leader.

Participation in the Cultural Events

Every year, the Kureiphula troupe starts performing from the month of November to May in various occasions, namely Nua Khaai, Pausa Punei, Baali Mahotsava, Mandei of Nabarangpur and Dhanujaatra. The Baaja *dal* performs mostly in Car Festivals, Kalahandi Utsav and Nua Khai (state level). It is depicted from the Table 2.4 that these two troupes have performed in village, Panchayat, Block and district levels under the sponsorship of the respective cultural authority. For these performances, they have not received neither any monetary support nor benefits. Since 1990, the Maa Mangala Troupe has been participating in Dusehra and Durga Puja up to district level. In some of these events they were awarded with prize and cash money (Rs. 200 to Rs. 400).

Expectations

All the three troupes desired for government assistance and patronization for their folk dance forms. They also seemed to need good road and infrastructure in their villages. Each troupe also has a requirement for a club-house to sustain their activities.

Majhiguda Gram Panchayat

Jaya Madhab Banabaari Club is the only troupe representing this Gram Panchayat. Krushidhara Bag is the founder and President of this troupe. This troupe consists of 14 male members constituting SC (8) and OBC (6). The trainee has to undergo the training for two months in the village. The main objective of this troupe is to worship Lord Krishna, Lord Balaram and Arjuna.

Theme

This is a traditional folk dance of Gauda community. They compose devotional songs for their performances. Through their folk dance they convey the message to the public that they are kith and kin (*sakha*) of Lord Shri Krishna. During performances, the villagers are also welcome to participate.

Costumes and Jewellery

They use attire similar to the troupes of Ampani Gram Panchayat. Apart from that, while dancing they use a stick which is made of Kendu tree.

Musical Instruments

The instruments used and played by this troupe and are also found to be similar to that of those used by the troupes of Ampani Gram Panchayat.

Participation in the Cultural Events

Their participation is only limited within the district level. They have participated in village Phagu Jatra, Bali Jatra and Kalahandi Cultural Utsav.

Expectations

The troupe desires for more attention and support from the Government. It also wants to perform in Adibasi Utsav at the State level in Bhubaneswar.

DudkaThenga Gram Panchayat

Three troupes, namely—Khaligarh Pujaari Pada Dal, Kaligada Pujari Para Dal and Maa Thakurani Dal Dandari have been identified as study troupes. The groups Kaligada Pujari Pada Dal and Khaligarh Pujari Para Dal are pure ST groups constituting seven Kandha members in each (Photograph 2.16). The troupes are of recent origin (4 years old). It has been recorded that the members of these troupes have been attending the troupe activities regularly. Whereas Maa Thakurani Dal constitutes nine male members belonging to SC (2 from Damba) and ST (7 from Bhatra) communities. This is the oldest troupe in this Gram Panchayat and since 1990 it has been performing. They only dance during Pausa Punei. Hence, their meetings are conducted only once in a year in the month of January.

Costumes and Jewellery

Items like saris, head gear, armlets, sleeveless coats, imitations, waist belt (*anta patti*), bangles (*kada*), *dhoti*, big earrings (*kundala*) are used by these two troupes. The total cost of their attire ranges between Rs. 400 to Rs. 500 (Table 2.2).

Musical Instruments

Khaligarh Pujari Dal and Kaligada Pujari Para Dal use five types of instruments, which are Nisan, Chamta, Tidibidi, Doodra and Sedrum. Tidibidi is a traditional instrument made of mud and goat skin and costs about Rs. 100. Sedrum, another instrument, is bought from a distant place Dabuguda of undivided Koraput district, which costs about Rs. 600. Rest of the instruments are bought from Dahigaan, a nearby locality. Maa Thakurani Dal possesses various instruments such as flute, Tidibidi, Ginni/Kubil and Jhumka that in totality costs about Rs. 500 (Table 2.3). These instruments are bought from Junagarh of Kalahandi district.

Participation in the Cultural Events

The Khaligarh Pujari Dal and Kaligada Pujari Dal participated in Pausa Purnima at the village level bearing the costs themselves. For their performance in the Koksara Block, the troupes earned Rs. 200 each. In January 2005, the troupes participated in Kalahandi Utsav (Ghumra 2005) under the sponsorship of district administration. They received monetary support of Rs. 500 for this event. Maa Thakurani Dal has been participating at village, Panchayat, Block and district levels for which it has received monetary support and grocery items.

Expectations

The requirements of these three troupes are similar to the needs of the troupes of Aampani Gram Panchayat.

Lanjigarh Block

The Lanjigarh Block is 48 km away from the district headquarters. A total number of 11 folk troupes have been identified from three Gram Panchayats namely—Lanjigarh, Chhatrapur and Trilochanpur. Among these eleven troupes, eight troupes are 'Dhap' performing groups while the rest three troupes belong to three different categories, namely—Ghumra, Sankirtana Dal and Folk Dance Party.

Ghumra Troupe

The only Ghumra party in this block is known as Maa Bhairabi Kala Kendra Ghumra Dal (Photograph 2.17). This troupe is 25 years old and constitutes 20 male members belonging to OBC (Paika) category. The founder of the troupe is Mr. Narayana Pradhan who is also called as the Guru. Being a Ghumra dance party, the theme, the objective, the jewellery, the costumes, the musical instruments etc. are found to be in similar trend of the Ghumra parties of Kalahandi District. However, a little variation has been observed in case of participation of the troupe in cultural events. It has been recorded that although the group is one of the oldest Ghumra troupes, it is yet to get any opportunity to represent itself in any important cultural events. The troupe has not even performed in Kalahandi Mahotsav, which is organized by district cultural committee of Bhawanipatna. As such, it has not yet performed at State level.

Agni Bhairabi Bajaa Party and Sankirtana Dal

The Agni Bhairabi Bajaa Party is a folk dance party and is composed of ten male members belonging to ST (Kandha) category (Photograph 2.18). The objective of the troupe is solely based on worshipping Goddess Agni Bhairabi for communal harmony. Whereas, the Sankirtana Dal is composed of 20 male members who all belong to OBC (Paika) community. The motto of this troupe is to create spiritualism and devotional feeling for Lord Krishna through chanting names of Lord Shri Krishna (*sankirtana*).

Costumes and Jewellery

Both the troupes wear attires which are quite similar to the attires worn by their counterparts of the other blocks which has already been illustrated (Table 2.2).

Musical Instruments

In case of instruments, these two troupes play traditional instruments, which are also in use by their counterparts of the district. But, in addition to the common instruments, the Sankirtana Dal has been using another instrument named as Ram Taali (wooden musical instrument) that costs about Rs. 200 each (Table 2.3).

Participation in the Cultural Events

It has been noted that both the troupes have been participating in various religious occasions, cultural festivals and marriages at the village, Panchayat, Block and district level (Table 2.4). The Agni Bhairabi Troupe is the only troupe of the Block to participate in marriage functions in other States such as Andhra Pradesh.

Expectations

When asked about their needs, the troupe members have mentioned that they are in need of new instruments, financial assistance, a club house, good infrastructure and hospital facility.

Dhap Parties

The *Dhap* dance is basically a tribal dance. Since time immemorial, the Kandhas have been practicing this traditional dance form. The speciality of this dance is that the dance is performed both during the marriage celebration and in honour of the outsiders/guests coming to the village. The theme of their song connotes that the *Dharti Maa* (Mother earth) should take care of the newly married couple. While performing, the dancers spontaneously compose the song as according to the situation and dance to the rhythm. Both male and female members practice this dance. There are 4 male Dhap troupes, 1 mixed Dhap troupe and 3 female Dhap troupes. Although, this form of dance has been practiced since ancient times but the Dhap troupes were formed in the post-independence era (Table 2.1). Remarkably, these troupes have been in existence since 20 to 30 years now and have retained their identity. The pure female Dhap parties are, namely Dhap Dance Party of Bhataguda, Dhap Dance Party of Khemundipadar and Dhap Dance Party of Ainthapadar each constituting five to ten female members. There is a mixed group of Dhap of Kanakadu composed of five male members and five female members (Photograph 2.12). The rest are purely male groups—Dhap dance party Goipita, Dhap dance party Leptaguda, Dhap dance party Ladanga and Dhap dance party Pheldanek each having ten male members. Except for Dhap dance party of Leptaguda, all other Dhap parties have members from ST (Kandha) category only. While, Dhap dance party of Leptaguda consists of only SC (Damba) members. It is presumed that the SC (Damba) people have been influenced by the ST (Kandha) people and have started practicing this Dhap dance, which was earlier, performed and practiced only by the Kandha Tribal people.

Costumes and Jewellery

Both the male and female practitioners use the modern attire such as *dhoti*, shirt, towel, *sari*, blouse, etc. The males do not use any kind of jewellery whereas the females use jewellery such as *khagla*, *ghika*, clip, anklet (*painri*), *katriya*, armlet, *bandira*, bangles which in total costs about Rs. 400 (Table 2.2).

Musical Instruments

Two instruments are chiefly used by the troupes. The traditional instrument is known as Dhap, a single membrane drum made up of *babool* wood and skin of monkey. It costs about Rs. 150. There is another instrument named as Ram Taali and it costs about Rs. 50 (Table 2.3).

Participation in the Cultural Events

The performances of all the Dhap troupes are limited to marriage occasions in their villages, Panchayats and Block level. They are yet to perform in the State level (Table 2.4).

Expectations

The dancers are in need of financial assistance and better costumes.

Narla Block

Narla Block is situated 30 km away from the district headquarters. There are in total eight folk troupes as identified and taken for the study. For the study, six Gram Panchayats have been covered. They are—Narla, Rupra Road, Tulapada, Mandel, Sargiguga and Kandel. The eight folk troupes belonging to this Block can be broadly categorized into three types which are—(a) Ghumra troupes, (b) Natak troupes, and (c) Sankirtana Dal. All the troupes of this Block contain only male members. No female participation has been recorded in any of these troupes.

Ghumra Troupes

Dharani Dhar Ghumra Committee (Rupra Road Gram Panchayat) and Majhali Para Ghumra Party (Rupra Road Gram Panchayat) are the two Ghumra troupes of this Block. They have ten to eleven ST (Kandha) male members in each. Both the troupes have been in existence for more than 30 years. The founders of the two troupes are Dalapati Majhi and Prahallada Sahu respectively. The objectives, themes, costumes, jewellery and the musical instruments of these troupes are similar to their counterparts from other Blocks of the district. Dharani Dhar Ghumra Committee has performed during Dusehra in the months of September and October at the village, Panchayat,

Table 2.4 : Participation of Troupes of Kalahandi District in Cultural Events

Name of the Block/ Folk troupes	Troupe's Participation Levels					
	GP	Block	District	State	National	International
1. Bhawanipatna Block						
(a) Ghumra (5 troupes)	5	4	3	2	2	1
(b) Folk Drama (2 troupes)	2	1	—	—	—	—
Total : 7 troupes	7	5	3	2	2	1
2. Dharamgarh Block						
(a) Folk Drama Dance party (8 troupes)	8	8	7	2	—	—
(b) Ghumra (1 troupe)	1	1	1	1	—	—
Total : 9 troupes	9	9	8	3	—	—
3. Koksara Block						
(a) Kureiphula Group	1	1	1	—	—	—
(b) Folk dance drama parties (6 troupes)	5	6	6	—	—	—
Total : 7 troupes	6	7	7	—	—	—
4. Lanjigarh Block						
(a) Ghumra (1 troupe)	1	1	1	—	—	—
(b) Dhap (8 troupes)	8	8	—	—	—	—
(c) Devotional Parties (2 troupe)	2	2	2	1	—	—
Total : 11 troupes	11	11	3	1	—	—
5. Narla Block						
(a) Ghumra (2 troupes)	1	1	1	—	—	—
(b) Mixed Troupes (6 troupes)	6	6	3	—	—	—
Total : 8 troupes	7	7	4	—	—	—

Table 2.4 Contd.

Name of the Block/ Folk troupes	Troupe's Participation Levels GP	Block	District	State	National	International
6. Th.Rampur						
(a) Ghumra (4 troupes)	4	3	3	1	1	1
(b) Dhap (3 troupes)	3	3	2	1	1	—
(c) Mixed Groups (3 troupes)	3	2	1	—	—	—
Total : 10 troupes	10	8	6	2	2	1
Grand Total : 52 troupes	50	52	36	10	6	2

Block and Nuapada district under the sponsorship of the respective Puja committees (Photograph 2.20). The artists have not received any financial package for the events. On the other hand the performances of Majhali Para Ghumra Party have been limited to Block level only. In one such performance at village level at Asuragarh Fort they were rewarded a cash prize of Rs. 3,000. The troupes desired for better costumes and light and sound arrangements as well as financial support for their performances.

Folk Drama Troupes (Natak Parties)

There are five folk drama troupes taken as study troupes. Sri Sri Singhabahini Jagadhatri Gananatya Troupe (Kandel Gram Panchayat) is the oldest (year of formation—1965) among all the troupes of this Block (Table 2.1) and was formed by the village committee. It constitutes of 8 OBC (Gauda and Paika) male members and 2 ST (Kandha) male members. Maa Majhigauri Natak Committee (Sargiguda Gram Panchayat) is the youngest among all the troupes of the Block and was formed in 2000 by Mr. Dhabaleshara Majhi. It has nine ST (Kandha) and eleven OBC members. Shri Rama Navami Committee (Narla Gram Panchayat) and Ram Leela Troupe of Asuragarh (Mandel Gram Panchayat) have been performing since three decades. Ram Leela Troupe consists of 20 ST members. Shri Rama Navami Committee and Birata Parva Party of Badapada (Tulapada Gram Panchayat), besides having members from OBC and ST category, also have representatives from the General category. The objectives of these folk drama troupes are (a) to spread message of unity and integrity and to continue their folk traditions, (b) to preserve the heritage of folk drama, and (c) to promote their art forms. To meet these objectives, they undergo training under the teaching of their respective *gurus*. The themes of these troupes are based on mythological epics and piety for the village deities.

Costumes, Jewellery and Musical Instruments

The attires worn by these troupes are strikingly similar to those worn by other folk drama troupes of the Block. The accessories used by these troupes vary according to their themes. In case of musical instruments, these troupes also follow the general trends of other troupes of the Block.

Participation in Cultural Events

The Birata Parba Party has participated in many events such as Durga Puja, Laxmi Puja, etc. at the Block level and have also earned monetary gains of about Rs. 4,000 (Photograph 2.21). Shri Rama Navami Committee is yet to participate outside their village. Rest of the troupes have participated in village, Panchayat, Block or district levels.

Expectations

The basic requirements as mentioned by the performers are provision for better light and sound facilities for enhancing their performances. Besides, they also desire for new modern musical instruments and new themes for their folk dramas.

Sankirtana Dal

The only Sankirtana troupe of the Block is Jaga Balia Sankirtana Mandal (Mandel Gram Panchayat) and is newly founded (year

2000) by Mr. Basanta Kumar Nayak and Mr. Bijay Kumar Majhi. It constitutes of 15 male members who belong to OBC (Gauda, Kulthia) category. The theme of this troupe is to worship Lord Jaganath and spread spiritualism among the folk/rural mass. The objective of this troupe is to keep up the tradition.

Costumes, Jewellery and Musical Instruments

The troupe possesses and uses the same kind of costumes, jewellery and musical instruments as the other Sankirtana parties of the Block. There is negligible deviation in the continuing trend.

Participation in Cultural Events

This troupe has performed in village, Panchayat, Block and district level at various occasions of Kartika Purnima, naming ceremony of new borns, Asthaprahari *yagna* (held in February, March and April) etc. sponsored by the respective cultural committee. The troupe has not earned any major financial benefits out of these performances. They have visited other districts, namely—Koraput, Bolangir and Sambalpur. For these, they have received certain amount of cash (Rs. 400 to Rs. 500).

Expectations

The only concern of this troupe is to be able to get more financial assistance from different sources.

Thuamul Rampur Block

Thuamul Rampur is situated at a distance of 73 km from the district headquarters. A total number of ten folk dances from four Gram Panchayats (Th. Rampur, Gunupur, Kanigumma and Gopalpur) have been identified and taken into account for the study. The troupes can be broadly divided into Ghumra troupes (4), Salap Nishan (1), Dhap parties (3), and Folk dance parties (2).

Ghumra Troupes

The Ghumra troupes constitute six to twelve male members with majority of them belonging to OBC community and it has been recorded that each troupe has its respective Guru. The theme, objective, costumes and jewellery are found to be in similar trend as of their counterparts in other Blocks. Only variation has been found in case of the musical instruments and the level of participation. Lankeshwari (Gunupur Gram Panchayat) is the oldest troupe (34 years old). It has only participated up to the Block level Ghumra competition organized on Bali Jatra event and Dusehra festivals. However, the troupe has got the financial support of Rs. 1,000 for this trip and was awarded with first prize. Maa Manikeshwari troupe (Th. Rampur Gram Panchayat), a decade old, has availed the opportunity of participating in all the levels upto international level. It is revealed from the Table 2.4 that it has participated in Kalahandi Utsav and Bali Jatra event organized at the village Gram Panchayat and district levels with proper monetary support (TA/DA). by the respective cultural committee. In January 2001, it has participated in D.P.E.P programme at Puri under the sponsorship of D.P.E.P. with TA/DA. During the trip, the troupe got the chance to visit the Jaganath Temple. During April 1998, it participated in national level festival of Kumbha Mela Mahotsava at Haridwar with TA/DA under the sponsorship of National Youth and Cultural Committee. It has also participated in the World Trade Fair during 2002 November under IPR Department of Government of Orissa with TA/DA. The Kanigumma Ghumra Party (Kanigumma Gram Panchayat) has also participated in Kalahandi Utsav organized at Block and district level sponsored by village committee and Mahavira Sanskrutika Anushthana in November-December-January 2002-03. However, they have not received any financial support. Maa Thakurani Troupe (Gunupur Gram Panchayat) is a younger troupe (six to seven years of formation) is yet to get any privilege of participation outside their village level. The chief reason behind this is found to be their lack of information about the cultural events.

Musical Instruments

Maa Manikeshwari troupe only uses Ghumra (single membraned drum with two sticks). So, the whole troupe is known as 'Ghumrawala'. Each of the members possesses Ghumra individually and the maintenance costs are beared by the respective members. The Lankeshwari troupe possesses both Ghumra, Jhallar (peacock feathers) and Nisan (drum). Maa Thakurani Dal has seven instruments, namely—Tashawalla, Dolina, Jhumka, Nisan, Jhallar, Mahuri and Ghumra. Kanigumma Ghumra Party owns Ghumra, Jhallar, Nisan and Jhanjha.

Dhap/Dhab Parties

In the Block, the Dhap dance is also known as 'Dhab'. Three Dhap parties have been identified and taken as study groups. They are Brundabati Dal and Madingraja Dhap party (both belonging to Gunupur Gram Panchayat) and Dhap Dance party of Sargiguda (Gopalpur Gram Panchayat). These troupes are mixed groups constituting equal number of male and female members in each troupe. It has been recorded that there are limitations of memberships between 10 to 20 in each troupe. Regarding group formation there has been no record of any particular date or year of formation as these groups have been practicing for generations.

The troupes are named after the instrument 'Dhap' (single membraned drum). Besides Dhap, another instrument known as Ram Tali is also played. In a Dhap group, as a common practice, the young unmarried boys and girls of different villages dance together. The reason behind it is that both the Clan and village exogamy are followed strictly. While performing, the boys and girls stand facing each other and question each other in the form of musical notes. The replies are also given with equal spirit and spontaneity in the same manner. As a general trend, the contents are found to be based on prayers of village deity, marriage queries, jokes, riddles, man-woman relationship and nature, etc.

Brundabati Dal : It has ten ST (Kutiya Kandha) and two SC (Damba) members.The female members of this troupe play Ram Tali while the Dhap is played by the male members. With regard to costume, jewellery and theme, they share the general trend. The troupe has participated only in the district level events.

Madingraja Dhap Party : It is a pure ST group having 20 members. The male members play the Dhap and are known as 'Dhabwala'. They are yet to participate in any major event (Photograph 2.22).

Dhap Dance Party of Sargiguda (Photograph 2.23) : It has six ST (Kutiya Kandha), two SC (Damba) and two OBC (Paika). They play the Dhap and is the only Dhap troupe of this Block which has participated in village, Gram Panchayat and Block level during Laxmi and Durga Puja and Kalahandi Mahotsava (January 2002) under the sponsorship of district cultural organization.

Folk Dance Parties

Maa Thakurani Sanskrutika Kala Parishada and Khandarla Nacha Party (both belonging to Gunupur Gram Panchayat) are of recent origin (year of formation 2005). Maa Thakurani Sanskrutika Kala Parishada is formed by Hazinga Majhi and constists of twelve male members—six ST (Sabara) and six SC (Damba). Khandarla Nacha Party has 8 male members—five ST (Kandha) and three SC (Damba) (Photograph 2.24).

The costumes, jewellery and musical instruments are same as their contemporaries. No major participation has been done by the troupes at district level.

Salap Nishan

Salap Nishan dance troupe (Gunupur Gram Panchayat) is named after the respective musical instrument 'Salap nishan' (A big single membraned drum). Like Dhap, this is an ancient form of dance and constitutes only ten male members (SC—5, ST—2 and OBC—3). The objective of the dance is to keep up the traditional heritage as well as communal harmony. Besides, it is a martial dance played by both the tribal and non-tribal people. In case of their costumes, they do not differ much from other troupes. But they do not use any kind of jewellery.

Musical Instrument

The Salap Nishan is a big drum/dhol, which is played by two or three members of the troupe at the same time, and the dancers and singers perform in coordination with the drum beats. The instrument is traditional and made by the troupe members. It is made up of iron, cattle skin. The total cost sums up to about Rs. 1,500 (Table 2.3).

Participation

It has participated at village level. Also, it is found out that it also performed once in Kalahandi Mahotsava.

Overall Participation of Sample Troupes in Cultural Events of Kalahandi District

It is seen from Table 2.4 that a total number of 52 troupes have given performance in the Gram Panchayat level. All the troupes have also been able to perform at the Block level competition. On the contrary, only 36 troupes have given performance in the district level competitions, namely Kalahandi Mahotsava organized at Bhawanipatna. Amongst them, 10 troupes have availed the opportunity to present their dance form at the State level, Bhubaneswar. However, only six troupes have participated in the National level competition held at Delhi. Even two troupes had been on a dance trip to attend the international competitions. When we look into the troupe-wise participation at various levels, it is found that only the Ghumra troupes of all the six Blocks, and two folk drama troupes of Dharamgarh Block have been able to present their performances at the State level. As regards the international competition, Ghumra parties of Th. Rampur and Bhawanipatna Blocks have attended the international event organized at World Trade Fair during the year 2002.

Dying Folk Dances and Instruments of Kalahandi District

There are certain folk dances of this district, which are not practiced any more and hence are in dying state. Block-wise identification of such troupes was done through the interviews of different troupes from the six Blocks.

Bhawanipatna Block

(a) *Kichakabadha Folk drama* : Older generations are no more alive to teach the younger generations. The youngsters are also not keen to perform this art form.
(b) *Hirabati Haran* : The reason for its extinction is the same as above.
(c) *Subhadra Haran* : Younger artists do not take interest in this mythological theme.
(d) *Ganga Devi Natak Dal* : All the artists became old and expired. Hence, the group was disintegrated.
(e) *Lankapodi and Sitaharan* : Younger generation do not take interest in this art form.

Dharmagarh Block

(a) *Nagapada Arjuna Natak Dal* : The group broke because of conflicts among the members.
(b) *Maa Manikeshwari Dal* : Audience did not appreciate the performance and the troupe was discouraged to perform any more.

Lanjigarh Block

(a) *Patrapada Sankirtana Dal* : The troupe was disintegrated due to misunderstandings among its members.
(b) *Pujari Pada Natak Party* : Members could not give time for the practice. Hence, the folk form is in dying state.
(c) *Agni Bharaibi Natak Party* : Some of the members are old now, some have expired and youngsters are not interested to carry forward the folk tradition.
(d) *Solaboida* : The artists are no more alive to perform.

Th. Rampur Block :

(a) *Khanduan Troupe* : The troupe broke because of inter-rivalry among its members.

Musical Instruments : Similarly, certain traditional musical instruments are no more used. These are listed as below :

- *Sankha* : Conches are no more used due to non-availability.
- *Singh Baja* : It is an instrument which thorns attached to a single membrane drum and two artists had to simultaneously operate the drum. It is not used by Ghumra artists anymore due to the risk involved in playing the instrument because of the thorns. Government of Orissa has also banned this instrument.
- *Khanjani* : It is not widely used because of lack of availability of Iguana skin.
- *Maadala* : It is single membrane musical instrument made up of monkey skin and is played by Ghumra artists. This instrument is not used widely because of non-availability of monkey skin.
- *Timtin* : This instrument is no more in use as the audience did not appreciate its sound.
- *Dhola* : It is in dying state because it is found difficult by the artists to coordinate this instrument with other musical instruments.

Photographs

Photograph 2.1 : Bharati Ghumra Troupe of Bhawanipatna Block (one of the oldest troupes)

Photograph 2.2 : Training Place (*mandap*) of Ghumra Troupe of Bhawanipatna

Photograph 2.3 : Ghumra Instruments hanged carefully when not in use

Photograph 2.4 : Leading of Ghumra Troupes in *'Chhattar'* procession during Dusehra, Bhawanipatna

Photograph 2.5 : Manikeshwari Deity in 'Chhattar' procession, Bhawanipatna

Photograph 2.6 : Maa Manikeshwari Ghumra Dal of Th. Rampur Block with instruments

Photograph 2.7 : Training Place of Ghumra Troupes at Dharmagarh Block

Photograph 2.8 : Modern Instruments of Ghumra Troupe of Dharmagarh Block

Photograph 2.9 : Participation of Maa Manikeshwari Sanskrutika Anushthana Troupe at block level competition (Dharmagarh)

Photograph 2.10 : One member of Kuturu Baja Party of Dharmagarh Block

Photograph 2.11 : Participation of Folk Drama Troupe at Block Level Competition, Dharmagarh

Photograph 2.12 : Participation of Dhap Mixed Group of Kanakadu (Lanjigarh) Troupe at District Level Kalahandi Utsav

Photograph 2.13 : Jaya Madhaba Banabaadi Club of Koksara

Photograph 2.14 : Participation of Baja Dal of Budharaaja Sanskrutika Anushthana (Koksara Block) at Block Level Competition

Photograph 2.15 : Participation of Kureiphula Troupe at Kalahandi Utsav at district level

Photograph 2.16 : Two members of Maa Mangala Dal of Koksara

Photograph 2.17 : Kaligada Pujari Pada Dal of Koksara with Instruments

Photograph 2.18 : Maa Bhairabi Kala Kendra Ghumra Troupe of Lanjigarh Block

Photograph 2.19 : Agni Bhairabi Bajaa Dance Party of Lanjigarh Block

Photograph 2.20 : Participation of Dharani Dhar Ghumra Party of Narla Block at Nuapada District

Photograph 2.21 : Participation of Biraata Parba Party of Narla Block at District Level Kalahandi Utsav

Photograph 2.22 : Female Dhap Dance Party of Sargiguda, Th. Rampur Block

Photograph 2.23 : Madingraja Dhap Party of Th. Rampur Block

Photograph 2.24 : A Member of Khandarla Nacha Party of Th. Rampur performing during a marriage function

3

Socio-Economic Status of Folk Troupes

This chapter deals with the socio-economic status of the folk artists of the Kalahandi district. The concept of economic development primarily revolves round human resource in conjunction with exploitation of the natural resources. The need to view the economic and social development in a sustainable manner by enhancing the capacities of the people to use these resources in such a manner that it will generate additional income and employment for further development. With this background the section on socio-economic profile of the folk artists, which is closely related to overall growth of the concerned area, the Kalahandi district in general.

Age-wise Distribution of Troupe Members

Out of the total 52 sample troupes constituting 686 members in total, 67 are under the age-group of 10 to 17 years, which accounts for 9.77 per cent of the total membership (Table 3.1). On the other hand, there are 286 members within the age group of 18 to 25 years, which accounts for 41.69 per cent of the total membership. It is also revealed from the table that there are also elderly troupe members within the age brackets of 26 to 31 and 32 to 50 above, who constitute 25.22 per cent and 20.69 per cent respectively in Kalahandi district.

This, however, gives different pictures if we consider individual Block status. The Bhawanipatna Block shares similar pattern in age-wise distribution as of the overall age-group distribution among its troupe members. However, Dharamgarh Block projects a different profile with maximum number of

Table 3.1 : Distribution of Folk Artists according to Age-Groups and Marital Status in the Study Blocks of Kalahandi District

Sl. No./GP	*Name of group/Troupe*	*Marital Status*		*Age Distribution*			
		Married	*Unmarried*	*10-17*	*18-25*	*26-31*	*32-50*
	Bhawanipatna Block						
1. Sadar GP	Bharati Ghumra Dal (20)	6	14	—	10	2	8
2.	Jaya Maa Bhawani Group (18)	6	12	3	8	3	4
3.	Ghumra Karunda Kala Kendra (16)	8	8	2	8	—	6
4.	Mahavir Sanskrutika Anushthan Ghumra group (20)	12	8	—	1	8	11
5.	Sri Sri Balagopal Anushthana (10)	8	2	—	6	2	2
6. Medinipur GP	Sri Chaitanya Sanskutika Dal (10)	8	2	—	3	3	4
7. Gadalipadar GP	Thakurani Gananatya (20)	10	10	3	10	3	4
Total-7	114	58	56	8	46	21	39
%age	100	50.87	49.13	7.02	40.35	18.42	34.21
	Dharmagarh Block						
1.Kharipadar GP	Sri Krishna Yuvak Sangha Prem Sankritana Dal (12)	12	—	—	3	3	6
2.	Kharipadar Nacha Party (22)	22	—	4	6	9	3
3.	Mere Sarabadha (25)	25	—	4	6	7	8
4.	Phulana Sundari Behrapara Natak Party (20)	20	—	—	5	9	6
5. Chhilpa GP	Kuturu Baja Party (12)	12	—	1	4	4	3
6.	Duarsani Sanskrutika Kala Parishad (20)	20	—	—	2	—	18
7.	Ramaleela Geeti Natya (20)	20	—	—	3	8	9
8.	Maa Manikeswari Sanskrutika Anushthana (10)	10	—	1	3	3	3

9.	Maa Thakurani Baja Saala (6)	6	—	—	2	3	1
Total-9	147	147	—	10	34	46	57
%age	100	100	0	6.80	23.13	31.29	38.78
	Koksara Block						
1. Ampani GP	Kureiphul Group of Budha Raja Sanskrutika Anushthana, Ampani (12)	7	5	4	6	2	—
2.	Bajadala of Budha Raja Sanskrutika Anushthana (10)	8	2	2	7	1	—
3.	Maa Mangala Dal, Mandili (11)	7	4	3	3	4	1
4. Majhiguda GP	Jai Madhava Banabari Club (14)	14	—	—	5	8	1
5. Dudka Thenga GP	Khaligarh Pujhari Para Dal (7)	1	6	5	1	1	—
6.	Maa Thakuri Dal, Dandari Khaligarh (9)	7	2	2	2	1	4
7.	Kaligada Pujhari Para Dal (7)	1	6	5	2	—	—
Total-7	70	45	25	21	26	17	6
%age	100	64.29	35.71	30	37.14	24.29	8.57
	Lanjigarh Block						
1. Lanjigarh GP	Maa Bhairabi Kala Kendra Ghumura Dala (20)	17	3	3	12	4	1
2.	Agni Bhairabi Baja Party (10)	10	—	—	2	4	4
3.	Sankirtana Dal (20)	20	—	—	9	8	3
4.	Dhap Dance Party, Goipita (10)	10	—	—	6	3	1
5. Chhatarpur GP	Dhap Dance Party, Bhataguda (10)	7	3	—	9	1	—
6.	Dhap Dance Party, Leptaguda (10)	10	—	1	8	1	—
7. Trilochanpur GP	Dhap Dance Party, Khemundipadar (5)	5	—	2	3	—	—
8.	Adibasi Female Folk Dance, Ainthapadar (10)	7	3	4	3	3	—

Sl. No./GP	Name of group/Troupe	Marital Status		Age Distribution			
		Married	Unmarried	10-17	18-25	26-31	32-50
9.	Adibasi Male Folk Dance, Kanakadu (10)	7	3	3	5	2	—
10.	Dhap Dance Party, Ladanga (10)	10	—	3	4	3	—
11.	Dhap Dance Party, Pheldanek (10)	4	6	2	7	1	—
Total-11	125	107	18	18	68	30	9
%age	100	85.6	14.4	14.4	54.4	24	7.2
	Narla Block						
1. Narla GP	Sri Ram Navami Committee (10)	10	—	—	5	4	1
2. Rupra Road GP	Dharani Dhar Ghumura Committee (10)	10	—	—	5	3	2
3.	Majhali Para Ghumura Party (11)	11	—	1	8	2	—
4. Tulapada GP	Birat Parva Party, Badapada (20)	20	—	—	5	14	1
5. Mandel GP	Ram Leela Troupe, Ashuragarh (20)	20	—	—	2	10	8
6.	Jaga Balia Sankirtan Madala (15)	15	—	—	7	7	1
7. Sargiguda GP	Maa Majhigauri Natak Committee (20)	20	—	3	13	4	1
8. Kandel GP	Sri Sri Singhabahini Jagadhatri Gana Natya (10)	10	—	—	9	1	—
Total-8	116	116	—	4	54	45	13
%age	100	100	0	3.45	46.55	38.8	11.21
	Thuamul Rampur Block						
1. Th. Rampur GP	Maa Manikeswari Dal (12)	6	6	—	10	2	—
2. Gunupur GP	Salap Nishan (10)	8	2	—	8	1	1
3.	Lankeswari Ghumura Party (12)	5	7	—	9	2	1
4.	Maa Thakurani Sanskrutika Kala Parishad (12)	8	4	8	4	—	—

5.	Khandarla Nacha Party (8)	8	—	6	2	—	—
6.	Brundabati Dal (12)	7	5	3	6	2	1
7.	Maa Thakurani Dal, Harijan Pada (6)	6	—	—	—	—	6
8.	Madingaraja Dhap Party (20)	18	2	4	5	4	7
9. Kanigumma GP	Kanigumma Ghumura Dal (12)	5	7	1	9	1	1
10.Gopalpur GP	Dhap Dance Party, Sargiguda (10)	9	1	2	5	2	1
Total-10	114	80	34	24	58	14	18
%age	100	70.2	29.8	21.1	50.9	12.3	15.8
Grand Total-52	686	553	133	67	286	173	142
Overall %age	**100**	**80.61**	**19.39**	**9.77**	**41.69**	**25.22**	**20.69**

members (57) belonging to the age group of 32 to 50 years and above, which accounts 38.78 per cent of the total of 147 troupes members of the Block. In case of Koksara and Lanjigarh Blocks, Table 3.1 depicts a different profile in which there are only 8.57 per cent and 7.2 per cent members under the age group of 32-50 years respectively. It also indicates the inclination of more number of younger people towards folk dances, as these Blocks constitute 21 per cent and 18 per cent members respectively from the age group of 10 to 17 years. The Narla and Th. Rampur Blocks present the maximum membership trend from the young people under the age group of 18 to 25 years, which accounts to 46.55 and 50.9 per cent respectively.

Marital Status

There is a definite impact of marital status both on the performance level and economic aspect of the folk troupes. An analysis of the field data on overall marital status reveals that a majority of troupe membership accounts for married members which constitute 80.61 per cent in comparison of the total 686 members to unmarried members constituting only 19.39 per cent (Table 3.1). It is perceived from Table 3.1 that married people with family responsibility are still in touch with their traditional form of folk dance. However, an inclination of unmarried younger mass towards their respective folk practices is also witnessed. As regards the marital status of the troupe members of the individual Blocks, it is found from the Table 3.1 that Bhawanipatna, Koksara, Lanjigarh and Th. Rampur blocks convey the same status as of the overall marital status of all the troupe members of the district. But to the exception, the data collected from the two Blocks, namely Dharamgarh and Narla illustrates that the troupe membership of these two Blocks are completely credited by married members.

Educational Status of Folk Artists

The distribution of artists and their educational achievements reflect that only 23.03 per cent are illiterate among the total

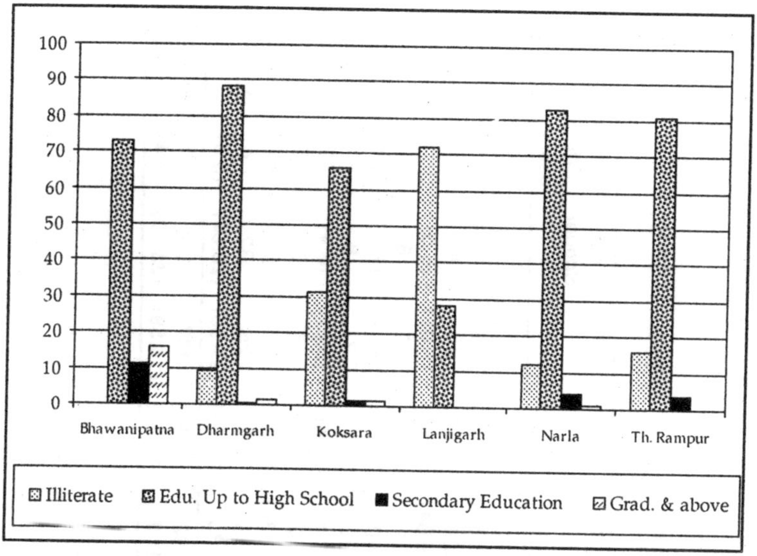

Graph 3.1 : Educational Status of Folk Artists of the Study Blocks of Kalahandi District (in %)

686 members (Table 3.2) in the district. On the other hand, a majority of members (70.24%) share a higher status in formal educational achievement. This again shows that majority of members have attended their school education. This shows that irrespective of the educational status, the folk population of the district continues to have an inclination towards their respective folk dance and music. It is depicted from Table 3.2 that except Lanjigarh Block troupes, rest five Blocks have members with secondary education. Further, it is seen from the Table that only few members (3.49%) of the 52 troupes have attained secondary education (Graph 3.1).

Occupational Status of the Folk Artists

The distribution of troupe members on the basis of their occupation has been given in Table 3.3. It is observed from Table 3.3 that a major portion of 51.31 per cent of the total members (686) is dependent on daily wage whereas 24.19 per cent members of the district are engaged in the agriculture as sector given in (Table 3.3). Table 3.3 denotes that out of the

Table 3.2 : Educational Status of Folk Artists of the Study Blocks of Kalahandi District

Name of the Block/No. of GPs	*No. of Troupes*	*Total No. of Members*	*Illiterate*	*LP*	*UP*	*ME*	*High School*	*Secondary Education*	*Grad. and above*
Bhawanipatna/3	7	114 **(100)**	— (0)	12 (10.53)	16 (14.04)	12 (10.53)	43 (37.72)	13 (11.40)	18 (15.79)
Dharmagarh/2	9	147 **(100)**	14 (9.52)	28 (19.04)	35 (23.81)	25 (17.01)	42 (28.57)	1 (0.68)	2 (1.36)
Koksara/3	7	70 **(100)**	22 (31.43)	7 (10)	18 (25.71)	13 (18.57)	8 (11.43)	1 (1.43)	1 (1.43)
Lanjigarh/3	11	125 **(100)**	90 (72)	8 (6.4)	12 (9.6)	7 (5.6)	8 (6.4)	— (0)	— (0)
Narla/6	8	116 **(100)**	14 (12.07)	12 (10.34)	28 (24.14)	25 (21.55)	31 (26.72)	5 (4.31)	1 (0.86)
Th. Rampur/4	10	114 **(100)**	18 (15.79)	15 (13.2)	20 (17.54)	25 (21.93)	32 (28.07)	4 (3.51)	— (0)
Total in Kalahandi District : (No. of Blocks-6 and No. of GPs-21)	**52**	**686 (100)**	**158 (23.03)**	**82 (11.95)**	**129 (18.80)**	**107 (15.59)**	**164 (23.90)**	**24 (3.49)**	**22 (3.20)**

Note : Figures in brackets indicate percentage.

Table 3.3 : Occupational Status of Folk Artists of the Study Blocks of Kalahandi District

Name of the Block/No. of GPs	*No. of troupes*	*Total No. of members*	*Skilled Labour*	*Daily Wage Labour*	*Agri-Labour*	*Businessmen*	*Govt. Service*	*Student*
Bhawanipatna/3	7	114 **(100)**	46 (40.35)	31 (27.2)	5 (4.4)	12 (10.53)	11 (9.65)	9 (7.89)
Dharamgarh/2	9	147 **(100)**	21 (14.29)	70 (47.62)	48 (32.65)	2 (1.36)	5 (3.40)	1 (0.68)
Koksara/3	7	70 **(100)**	9 (12.86)	20 (28.57)	33 (47.14)	3 (4.29)	— (0)	5 (7.14)
Lanjigarh/3	11	125 **(100)**	7 (5.6)	117 (93.6)	— (0)	— (0)	— (0)	1 (0.8)
Narla/6	8	116 **(100)**	6 (5.17)	72 (62.07)	28 (24.14)	6 (5.17)	4 (3.45)	— (0)
Th. Rampur/4	10	114 **(100)**	13 (11.40)	42 (36.84)	52 (45.61)	1 (0.87)	4 (3.51)	2 (1.75)
Total in Kalahandi District : (No. of blocks-6 and No. of GPs-21)	**52**	**686 (100)**	**102 (14.87)**	**352 (51.31)**	**166 (24.19)**	**24 (3.49)**	**24 (3.49)**	**18 (2.62)**

Note : Figures in brackets indicate percentage.

total 686 troupe artists of the district, 14.87 per cent members are skilled labourers and it has been recorded that these members are busy in various skilled jobs, namely—electric repair work, plumber work, cycle repairing and garage workshops. Again, it is learnt from the Table that there are few members working in government sector (3.49%) and business sector (3.49%). However, the troupe members of the Lanjigarh Block show a different occupational status with 95 per cent members working as skilled and daily wage labourers out of the Block's total number (125) of folk artists (Table 3.3). Interestingly, a student is also found to be one among 125 members of this Block.

The above discussion shows that this variation in occupations could have different socio-economic impacts in the pursuits of the folk dance activity, which has been subsequently discussed in the section related to the economic status of the folk artists of the district.

Economic Status of the Folk Artists

Possession of landed property and household assets reflect one's economic strength. Understanding this, an attempt has been made to account both the individual possession of landed property as well as of troupe's assets in order to know the net economic status of a folk artist. The details of the economic status are given in Table 3.4. It has been recorded that the folk artists possess various household items such as utensils and home appliances like radio, television etc. The troupe assets possessed by individual folk artists are mainly found to be costumes and jewellery and musical instruments. It is illustrated from Table 3.4 that net economic status of a folk actor of the Narla block is the highest among all the troupes, which constitute a major share of possession of landed property (82.57%) and livestock (7.46%). Again with regard to the troupe's assets, the Block shows highest share (2.83%) of its net economic status of possession of the musical instruments in comparison to the members of other Blocks. It is followed by the economic status of the artists of Bhawanipatna block (Rs. 85,583.60), which constitutes 80.77 per cent of landed property and highest percentage of household utensils (11.94%). The Table depicts that the net economic status of a Lanjigarh folk artist is quite poor (Rs. 35, 493.36) in the district. However, from the overall economic status it has been observed that a folk artist of Kalahandi district possesses 82.86 per cent of landed property, 14.62 per cent of household assets and 2.51 per cent of troupe assets out of his total economic strength in average (Table 3.4).

Annual Income

The household annual income of a folk artist (Graph 3.2) has been calculated taking into account of the income raised from both the major livelihood sources and folk dance. The major livelihood sources are agriculture and horticulture produces, Minor Forest Produces (MFP), wage earning and regular service. The average annual income of a folk artist of the Bhawanipatna block is recorded to be the highest income (Rs. 26,725.7) among the average annual incomes of folk artists of all other Blocks. The net income accounts 5.51 per cent share to folk dance, 5.63 per cent from MFP, 47.52 per cent of Agri/ Horticultural produce share and wage/daily-labour/service accounts for 41.34 per cent (Table 3.5). The folk artists of the Narla Block have the second highest income (Rs. 22,731.25) with highest possession of (56.09%) agricultural/horticultural produces (Table 3.5). Among all the Blocks, the folk artists of Koksara show the lowest annual income (Rs. 16,921.31) followed by Dharamgarh (Rs. 17,717.4) and Th. Rampur (Rs. 19,260). The folk artists of Th. Rampur and Lanjigarh Blocks owe maximum amount (85.05% and 59.83%) of their average annual income to daily wages respectively. It is again seen that except Narla, all other Blocks have forest produces as their economic source that accounts for 5.35 per cent of the average annual income of a folk artist of Kalahandi district. Although, the district comes under the government's KBK plan, the 100 days NEGs is yet to provide benefits to the folk artists as revealed from Table 3.5. On the whole, it is observed from the Table that on an average a folk artist of Kalahandi district annually earns Rs. 20,745.74 from various sources, namely folk

Table 3.4 : Economic Status of the Folk Artists of the Study Blocks of Kalahandi District (Per Household in Average)

Name of the Block/No. of GPs	*Landed Property (Value of House and Land) (in Rs.)*	*Cost of household assets*			*Cost of Troupe Assets*		***Net Economic Status of a folk artist (in Rs.)***
		Household utensils and home appliances (in Rs.)	*Agri implements (in Rs.)*	*Domestic Animals (in Rs.)*	*Musical instruments (in Rs.)*	*Jewellery and Costumes (in Rs.)*	
Bhawanipatna/3	69,128.57 (80.77)	10,221.7 (11.94)	432.85 (0.51)	4,871.42 (5.69)	689.7 (0.81)	239.42 (0.28)	85,583.66 **(100)**
Dharamgarh/2	34,822.22 (79.86)	3,117.22 (7.15)	555.56 (1.27)	3,854.4 (8.84)	734.67 (1.68)	520.56 (1.19)	43, 604.63 **(100)**
Koksara/3	44,583.3 (85.03)	2,230.5 (4.25)	532.6 (1.02)	3,713.3 (7.08)	917.5 (1.75)	454.6 (0.87)	52, 431.8 **(100)**
Lanjigarh/3	26,818.18 (75.56)	2,303.65 (6.49)	560.54 (1.58)	5,241.45 (14.77)	147 (0.414)	422.54 (1.19)	35,493.36 **(100)**
Narla/6	77,125 (82.57)	4,963.5 (5.31)	967.15 (1.04)	6,975.4 (7.46)	2,644.5 (2.83)	727.83 (0.78)	93,403.38 **(100)**
Th.Rampur/4	66,084 (92.04)	2,770.84 (3.86)	294.5 (0.41)	454.27 (0.63)	1,654.2 (2.30)	543.92 (0.76)	71,801.73 **(100)**
Average Economic Status of a folk artist of Kalahandi District	53,093.54 (82.86)	4,627.90 (7.22)	557.2 (0.87)	4,185.04 (6.53)	1,131.26 (1.76)	484.81 (0.75)	64,079.75 **(100)**

Note : Figures in brackets indicate percentage.

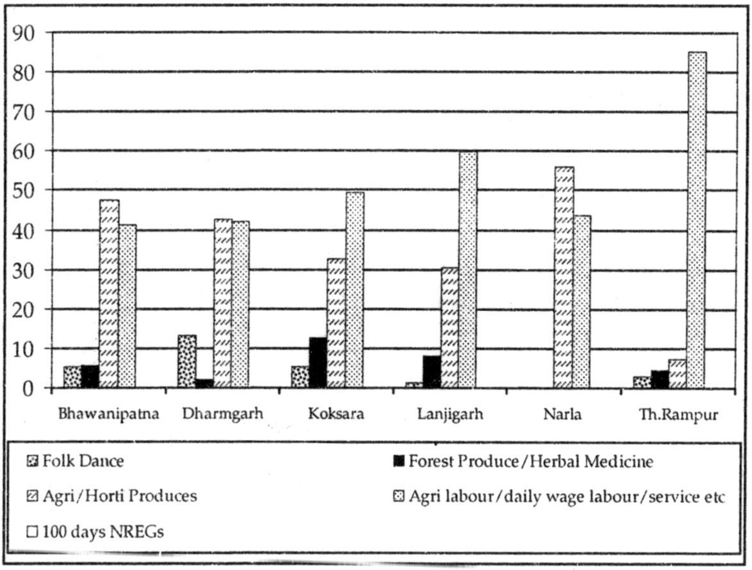

Graph 3.2 : Annual Income of a Folk Artist of the Study Blocks of Kalahandi District (in %)

dance (4.55%), MFP (5.35%), agricultural/horticultural produces (37.3%) and agricultural/daily/skilled labour and service (52.82%).

Annual Expenditure

It is observed that the higher the income level, lower is the percentage of income spent on consumption of food items. The National Sample Survey (NSS) throws light on consumer expenditure of families of different income levels separately for rural and urban areas. This is utilized for estimating the population under Below Poverty Line (BPL). For the analysis of annual expenditure of the folk artists indication of 'monthly per capita consumer expenditure' (MPCE), has been taken as the guiding factor for determining the economic status of the artists. Accordingly, a ratio of expenditure on food and non-food items have been taken into account as the indicators for identifying the standard of living of people. The food items include all the edible and the liquor beverages. On the other

Table 3.5 : Annual Income of Folk Artist of the Study Blocks of Kalahandi District (Per Study Household in Average)

Name of the block/ No. of GPs	*Folk Dance (in Rs.)*	*Forest/ Herbal Medicne (in Rs.)*	*Agri/ Horti Pro-duces (in Rs.)*	*Agri Labour/ Daily Labour/ Skilled Labour/ Service (in Rs.)*	*100 days NEGS (in Rs.)*	*Annual Income of a folk artist (in Rs.)*
Bhawanipatna/3	1,471.42	1,505.71	12,700	11,048.57	—	26,725.7
	(5.51)	(5.63)	(47.52)	(41.34)	(0)	**(100)**
Dharamgarh/2	2,344.4	388.88	7,555.55	7,428.57	—	17,717.4
	(13.23)	(2.19)	(42.64)	(41.93)	(0)	**(100)**
Koksara/3	892.85	2,142.75	5,528.57	8,357.14	—	16,921.31
	(5.27)	(12.66)	(32.67)	(49.39)	(0)	**(100)**
Lanjigarh/3	300	1,727.79	6,454.64	12,636.37	—	21,118.8
	(1.42)	(8.18)	(30.56)	(59.83)	(0)	**(100)**
Narla/6	81.25	—	12,750	9,900	—	22,731.25
	(0.36)	(0)	(56.09)	(43.55)	(0)	**(100)**
Th.Rampur/4	580	890	1,410	16,380	—	19,260
	(3.01)	(4.62)	(7.32)	(85.05)	(0)	**(100)**
Average Annual Income per house-hold in Kalahandi District	944.98 (4.55)	1,109.18 (5.35)	7,733.13 (37.3)	10,958.45 (52.82)	— (0)	20,745.74 **(100)**

Note : Figures in brackets indicate percentage.

hand, the non-food items includes all the household articles, costumes, medicines, utensils, education, tobacco and economic assets. It is observed (Table 3.6) that Bhawanipatna Block states the highest annual expenditure (Rs. 39,979) with 55.39 per cent of the net spent on food items and 44.61 per cent on non-food items. While, Lanjigarh Block accounts the lowest (Rs. 21,790) annual expenditure. Overall, the same ratio of expenditure on food and non-food items is seen in rest of the Blocks. This indicates that the folk artists of all the sample Blocks (6) fall within the category of BPL status. In general, a folk artist of Kalahandi district spends 59.36 of the net per cent (Rs. 20,745.74) spent on food items and 40.64 per cent on non-food items annually (Graph 3.3).

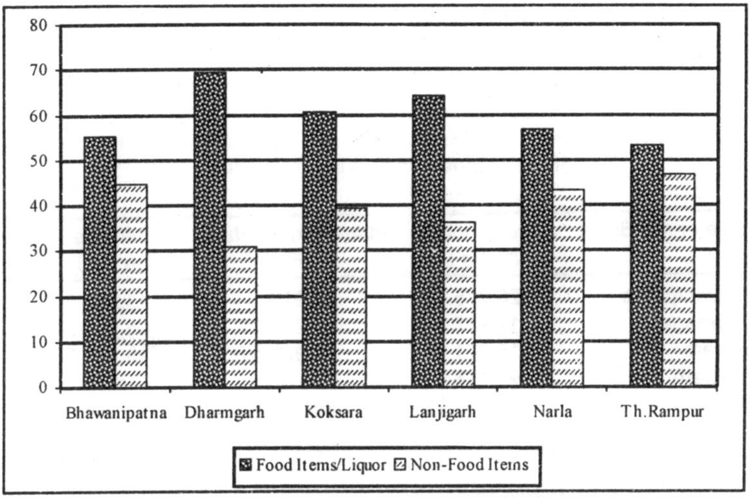

Graph 3.3 : Annual Expenditure of a Folk Artist of the Study Blocks of Kalahandi District (in %)

Table 3.6 : Annual Expenditure of a Folk Artist of Study Blocks (Per Study Household Consumption in Average)

Name of the Block	*Expenditure on food items (in Rs.)*	*Expenditure on non-food items (in Rs.)*	*Total Expenditure (in Rs.)*
Bhawanipatna	22,142.85 (55.39)	17,837.14 (44.61)	39,979 **(100)**
Dharmagarh	16,111.11 (69.21)	7,166.66 (30.79)	23,277.77 **(100)**
Koksara	19,428.57 (60.66)	12,600 (39.34)	32,028.57 **(100)**
Lanjigarh	13,954.54 (64.04)	7,836.36 (35.96)	21,790 **(100)**
Narla	14,875 (56.69)	11,362.5 (43.31)	26,237.5 **(100)**
Th. Rampur	12,550 (53.23)	11,025 (46.77)	23,575 **(100)**
Annual Expenditure of a folk artist of Kalahandi District	16,510.345 (59.36)	11,304.61 (40.64)	27,814.64 **(100)**

Note : Figures in brackets indicate percentage.

When we compare the annual ir :ome and expenditure if the folk artists of the respective Blocks, it is found that all the folk artists have to manage within a deficit budget (Table 3.7).

Table 3.7 : Comparison of Annual Income and Expenditure of a Folk Artist of Study Blocks in Kalahandi District

Name of the Block	*Annual Income (in Rs.)*	*Annual Expenditure (in Rs.)*	*Balance (in Rs.)*
Bhawanipatna	26,725.7	39,979	–13,253.3
Dharmagarh	17,717.4	23,277.77	–5,560.37
Koksara	16,921.31	32,028.57	–15,107.26
Lanjigarh	21,118.8	21,790	–671.2
Narla	22,731.25	26,237.5	–3,506.25
Th. Rampur	19,260	23,575	–4,315

Savings and Indebtedness

Indebtedness is the root cause of all the miseries of the tribal and rural folks. Due to lack of education and poor awareness level, the money lender in these areas, exploit the people. In spite of government's initiative on providing savings and credentials through post offices and banks, the rural people are still exploited by the local money lenders (*saahukars*). Considering these factors, the annual savings and indebtedness of the artists are taken into account for analysis. It has been recorded that the artists have taken loans from post offices and state banks for their personal purpose. (Table 3.8). The folk artists of Bhawanipatna and Narla Block have savings accounts in SBI and post offices. It is again found that they have availed loan facilities for purchasing agricultural implements, tractors with the prescribed banking loan facility whereas the blocks of interior areas such as Lanjigarh and Th. Rampur are more dependent on the money lenders than the banks and post offices. While taking into account of the overall saving status and indebtedness of the folk artists, it is revealed that the annual indebtedness (Rs. 1,608.38) is more than the annual savings (Rs. 472.17).

Table 3.8 : Annual Savings and Indebtedness of a Folk Artist in Each Study Block (in Average)

Name of the Block	*Annual Savings (in Rs.)*	*Annual Indebtedness (in Rs.)*
Bhawanipatna	314.28	4285.71
Dharmagarh	404.44	1777.7
Koksara	521.4	502.8
Lanjigarh	490.90	909.09
Narla	1,012	1,875
Th. Rampur	90	300
Average Savings and Indebtedness of a folk artist in Kalahandi district	472.17	1,608.38

Health Status

The diseases that are commonly prevalent in the study Blocks are malaria, jaundice, diarrhoea and skin disease. It has been recorded that the people take both the traditional and modern health care measures.

The interior areas of the respective Blocks are deprived of the provision of PHC facilities. The people of these areas generally depend on the government hospital located at Bhawanipatna district headquarters. However, the traditional health care facilities are provided by the village medicine men who provide herbal treatment for various diseases/elements, namely—snake bite, skin disease, bone alignment etc. Details of the herbal medicines used in Kalahandi district are given in Table 3.9.

Table 3.9 : Herbal Medicines used in Kalahandi District

Name of Disease	*Botanical Name of the Plant*	*Local Name*
Malaria	*Phyllanthus sirusi*	Bhuin amla
Common cold-fever	*Adhatoda Vesica* (leaf)	Basadolu
Diarrhoea/Dysentery	*Desmodium gangeticus* (leaf)	Latimarna
Fractures	*Tamarindus Indica* (seed)	Tetelmara
Arthritis/Rheumatism	*Tinospora Cordifolia* (stem)	Gulitula
Skin diseases	*Achyranthes aspera* (leaf)	Nihod palu
Cuts and injuries	*Cassia fistule* (leaf)	Phundeni
Snake Bite	*Raswolfia serpentina* (root)	Bhuin karna
Poison	*Calotropis procera* (latex)	Arka dolu
Delivery	*Cissampelos Pareira* (leaf)	Jungli bel

Political Awareness

It has been recorded that 90 per cent folk artists cast their votes during elections. When asked about their expectations from the political leaders, the artists have expressed their desires, which are mentioned as below :

- A PHC in their village
- A tourist centre
- Trading centre for forest produces
- Health care facilities
- Irrigation facilities
- Electrification of the village
- Provision of more tube wells
- New costumes and instruments
- Tribal improvement fund
- Cooperation from district cultural office
- Road communication
- Telephone connection
- A centre for practice of folk dance and music

Expected Economic Gain from Mass Awareness Programme

The artists are positive about the future of their dance forms. According to them, they can gain additional income from the various awareness programmes, provided they will be assigned for such programmes by the Government and Non-Government agencies. Their expected income are given in Table 3.10. It is observed from the Table that for a two-hour performance in the awareness programmes, namely AIDS, malaria, leprosy, family planning, literacy, safe water, immunization and other social causes. Their expected gains will be between Rs. 1,000 to Rs. 2,000 for each programme in addition to TA/DA from the respective authority/ organization.

Table 3.10 : Participation of Folk Troupes in Awareness Programmes

Sl. No.	*Awareness Programme*	*Ghumra charge amount (in Rs.)*	*Nacha Party charge amount (in Rs.)*	*Salap Nishan charge amount (in Rs.)*	*Ghadel-charge amount (in Rs.)*	*Dhap Dance charge amount (in Rs.)*
1.	AIDS	3000	5000	3000	3000	3000
2.	Malaria	2000	3000	200	1000	2000
3.	Leprosy	3000	2000	1000	2000	2000
4.	Family Planning	2000	2000	1000	1000	2000
5.	Literacy	1000	1000	2000	1000	1000
6.	Safe Water	2000	2000	2000	500	2000
7.	Immunization	1000	1000	1000	2000	2000

Government's and NGO's Incentives

The artists have said that they only avail BPL scheme under which they get 60 kg to 25 kg rice per month whereas other schemes, namely food for work, hundred days NEGS and NGOs intervention are yet to be beneficial for them.

The artists have expressed their difficulties, which are noted as below :

- Poverty;
- They feel uncomfortable while performing at the common festival gathering place within a short notice from the district cultural office; and
- While going to participate in the events they face problems in travel arrangements.

4

Viability of Eco-Tourism in Kalahandi District

Eco-tourism in a general connotation means management of local resources, Human and Natural, to promote tourism in the area in a sustainable manner. It allows visitors to learn about the environment of an area while maintaining the environments pristine state. Simultaneously, eco-tourism provides employment opportunities to the local community. This process in the long run will have a definite impact on the standard of living of the people of that respective locality. With this background, the chapter examines the potential factors of eco-tourism and provides information on feasibility of eco-tourism. The chapter also deals with the viability of eco-tourism in the area. It also presents the opinion of research persons, artists, hoteliers, travellers, Focus Group Discussion and Participating Rural Appraisal (PRA) findings.

Viable Factors

Kalahandi is enriched with archaeological findings, historical monuments, cultural and religious places. As one of the Western Orissa district, Kalahandi although is famous locally for Handicrafts, Precious Stones, Tribal Art and Crafts and Herbal Medicines but is hardly recognised in other parts of Orissa. Eco-tourism can be promoted in the Kalahandi region through these potential factors. The distribution of these items are found abundantly in the six study Blocks (Photograph 4.1).

It is seen from Table 2.1 that there are 52 folk troupes and twenty types of arts and craftworks (Tables 4.1, 4.4, 4.7, 4.10,

4.13 and 4.16) in Kalahandi district. The district is found to be abundant in herbal medicines (55 types). Besides, there are 34 types of minerals as has been recorded (Tables 4.2, 4.5, 4.8, 4.11, 4.14 and 4.17). Apart from these, there are 76 places of tourism of significance in the district (Tables 4.3, 4.6, 4.9, 4.12, 4.15 and 4.18) and these places have been categorically divided into tourism types, namely historical, religion, wild life, tribal and industrial types. There are cultural organizations (Government and voluntary) and the craft villages (stone and wood craft centres) which have certainly pivotal roles towards eco-tourism.

THE BLOCK-WISE TOURISM PROFILE OF THE KALAHANDI DISTRICT

BHAWANIPATNA BLOCK

Table 4.1 : Arts and Crafts

Arts and crafts/ Place	*Caste of the crafts-man*	*Source of raw material*	*Cost of raw material (Rs.)*	*Market values (Rs. Per Item)*	*Market for selling*	*Distance from District HQ (in km)*	*Public Aware-ness (in percent-age)*
Bamboo work of Sagada	Kandh (ST) and Damba (SC)	Local forest	Nil	5-20	Local weekly market and Bha-wani-patna	0-20	99
Pottery of B. Patna	Potters (Gauda)	Clay	Nil	4-50	Local weekly market and main market	0-15	99
Khapar for house roof	Potters (Kandh, Gauda and Damba)	Clay from the local area	Nil	2-5 per piece	On demand—door to door	0-15	99
Wooden works	OBC (Gauda)	Local forest	Nil	Rs. 2-1000	Weekly market	0-15	99

Table 4.2 : Natural Resources

Name of Medicinal plants	*Usages*	*Precious stones**	*Remarks*
Peepal	Multipurpose cure	Ketar mankar	*Gem stones are being collected by individuals and sold to traders clandestinely.
Aswaostha	-do-	Bhisma mani	—
Pudina (Mint)	—	Manikya (Diamond)	—
Haldi (Turmeric)	-do-	Panna	—
Tulasi (Basilious)	-do-	Neelam	—
Neemb (Neem)	-do-	Gomed	—
Bajramuli root	Fractures	—	—
Bisalyakarani	Cuts and wounds	—	—
Patal garuda	Snake bites	—	—
Aanla (Amla)	Multipurpose cure	—	—
Harida (Haridra)	-do-	—	—
Bahada	-do-	—	—
Ganga siuli	Malaria	—	—

Table 4.3 : Places of Tourism of Significance

Sl. No.	*Name*	*Tourism Significance*	*Distance from Dist. HQ (km)*	*Public awareness (in %)*
1.	King's Palace	Historical Place	0	100
2.	Durbar Hall	Historical Place	0	100
3.	Mahavir Sanskrutika Anushthan	Cultural Organisation	0	100
4.	Manikeswari Temple	Religious Place	0	100
5.	Jagânatha Temple	Religious Place	0	100
6.	Bhawani Sankar Temple	Religious Place	0	100
7.	Kali Temple	Religious Place	0	90
8.	Neelakantheswar temple	Religious Place	0	90
9.	Budheswar Temple	Religious Place	0	80
10.	Asha Sagar	Artificial Lake	0	100
11.	Phullri Jharan	Natural waterfall	18	99
12.	Jakham	Forest Deptt. Guest house	24	99
13.	Jamuna Sagar Dam	River Valley Project	14	88
14.	Ravandore	Pilgrimage	16	43
15.	Jugsaipatna	Pilgrimage	24	75

Table 4.3 Contd.

Sl. No.	Name	Tourism Significance	Distance from Dist. HQ (km)	Public awareness (in %)
16.	Dookri Chanchra waterfall	Natural waterfall		79
17.	Ret river valley	Scenic spot		
18.	Jatangpadar	River valley project	10	82
19.	Ghusurigudi waterfall	Waterfall		
20.	Karlapat Tiger Sanctuary	Reserve Tiger Sanctuary	35	85
21.	Dad Jhar	Picnic spot		77
22.	Bana Durga	Pilgrimage	15	67
23.	Sagada	Minor Irrigation Project, Picnic spot	17	99
24.	Pensur	Picnic spot	18	65
25.	Ubhei	Picnic spot	17	55
26.	Ujanti	Picnic spot	21	45

DHARMAGARH BLOCK

Table 4.4 : Arts and Crafts

Arts and crafts/ Place	Caste of the crafts-man	Source of raw material	Cost of raw material (Rs.)	Market values (Rs. Per Item)	Market for selling	Distance from District HQ (in km)	Public Aware-ness (in percent-age)
Teak Wood Carving of Khairi-padar (Craft Village)	ST (Kondh), SC (Damba) and OBC (Mali, Lohar, Gauda, Badhei)	Local Forest (Pro-curing through Forest Depart-ment)	1200-1500 per cft	50-thou-sands depend-ing on size and work	Market-ing th-rough Coope-ratives, Exhibi-tion and Exports	45	99
Wood works in Kibidi	ST	-do-	-do-	-do-	Local Market and Dist. HQ	49	73
Pottery of Kundela	OBC	Local	Nil	2-500	Local and weekly market	55	67
Hand woven Saree of Chichei-guda	OBC (Meher)	Juna-garh and Raipur	50-1000	90-500	Local and weekly Market	62	45

Table 4.5 : Natural Resources

Name of Medicinal plants	*Usages*	*Precious stones*
Tulusi	Multipurpose	Manikya
Agasti	Gynic problem	Alexandria
Dalimba (Pomgranate)	Loose motion, Multi-purpose	Berill
Haldi (Termeric)	-do-	Barnet
Simuli lata (Creper)	Hair care and skin care	Kakaneela
Sajana (Drum stick)	High BP and body ache, swellings	Gomedh
—	—	Panna

Table 4.6 : Places of Tourism of Significance

Sl. No.	*Name*	*Tourism of Importance*	*Distance from Dist. HQ (km)*	*Public awareness (in %)*
1.	Paradeswar Temple	Religious Place	45	99
2.	Tel and Hathi River Valley	Picnic spots	40	99
3.	Dakhineswari Kali Mandir	Religious place	47	92
4.	Bhim Khoja	Picnic spot	48	88

KOKSARA BLOCK

Table 4.7 : Arts and Crafts

Arts and crafts/ Place	*Caste of the crafts-man*	*Source of raw material*	*Cost of raw material (Rs.)*	*Market values (Rs. Per Item)*	*Market for selling*	*Distance from District HQ (in km)*	*Public Aware-ness (in percent-age)*
1. Kanda-garh Stone carving of Idols and statues	ST	Local, Bhuba-neswar, and Keonjhar	100-5000	300-10000	Market-ing through-out India	85	96
2. Terra cotta of Majhi-guda	OBC	Local	Nil	20-500	Local and weekly Market	88	67
3. Bamboo work of Ampani	ST, SC, OBC, GEN	Local	Nil	5-100	-do-	98	75

Table 4.8 : Natural Resources

Name of Medicinal plants	*Usages*	*Precious stones*
Amla	Multipurpose	Neelam
Payal garuda	-do-	Gomed
Bahada	-do-	Kakaneeli
Haridra	-do-	Byril
Aakaranti	-do-	Garnate
Arakha	-do-	Diamond
Bella	-do-	—
Bajra muli	-do-	—
Akanabindhi	-do-	—
Baidanka (Lentils)	-do- and Alopacia	—
Palasha	-do-	—
Barakoli (Berry)	-do-	—
Jammun (Black Berry)	-do-, High BP, Diabetic	—

Table 4.9 : Places of Tourism of Significance

Sl. No.	*Name*	*Tourism Importance*	*Distance from Dist. HQ (km)*	*Public awareness (in %)*
1.	Guda Handi cave	Pre Historic Cave	88	89
2.	Ampani Ghati	Picnic spot	98	89
3.	Budha Raja Dangar	Picnic spot	87	67
4.	Haldi Gudari	Picnic spot	85	62
5.	Dokri Chanchra	Picnic spot	88	55
6.	Karak Dam	Dam site	89	53
7.	Sahaj Khola	Wild life	85	65
8.	Khaligada	Wild life	89	65
9.	Ampani Bodhigaya	Religious place	95	54
10.	Budha Raja Temple	Religious Temple	86	67
11.	Sidheswar Temple	Religious Place	83	42
12.	Trinath Temple	-do-	89	35
13.	Budha Raja Yubak Sangha	Cultural Organisation	65	43

LANJIGARH BLOCK

Table 4.10 : Arts and Crafts

Arts and crafts/ Place	*Caste of the crafts-man*	*Source of raw material*	*Cost of raw material (Rs.)*	*Market values (Rs. Per Item)*	*Market for selling*	*Distance from District HQ (in km)*	*Public Aware-ness (in percent-age)*
1. Pottery	ST	Local	Nil	2-50	-do-	68	45
2. Bamboo work of Patra-pada	OBC and ST	Local	Nil	5-100	-do-	71	62
3. Rope making	ST, SC and OBC	Local	Nil	10-100	-do-	75	56

Table 4.11 : Natural Resources

Name of Medicinal plants	*Usages*	*Precious stones* and metals*	*Remarks*
1. Aswotha	Multipurpose	Diamond	—
2. Babul	Hair and Dental care	Zinc	—
3. Neema	Multipurpose	Aluminium	Bedanta Alumina Ltd. at Lanjigarh is utilising the natural resources
4. Harida	-do-	—	—
5. Bahada	-do-	—	—
6. Amla	-do-	—	—
7. Arakha	-do-	—	—
8. Zaiphala	-do-	—	—
9. Bhui-kakharu	-do-	—	—
10. Patal-garuda	Snake bite	—	—

Table 4.12 : Places of Tourism of Significance

Sl. No.	*Name*	*Tourism Importance*	*Distance from Dist. HQ (km)*	*Public awareness (in %)*
1.	Niyamgiri Mountain Range	Wild life/Herbal Medicine/ Kutia Kondha PTG Habitat	65	85
2.	Kidingi Mountain Range	-do-	72	84
3.	Kadli Ghat	Scenic spot	75	78
4.	Ladang Ghat	-do-	73	77
5.	Bansa Dhara	River Valley Project	78	82
6.	Reta River	-do-	79	83
7.	Dang Mundi	Picnic spot	60	75
8.	Sikkarkuppa	-do-	55	89
9.	Kudhisila	-do-	53	86
10.	Vedanta Alumina Ltd.	Industrial Area	75	99
11.	Jaganatha Temple	Religious place	65	77
12.	Anna Vairab Temple	-do-	63	78
13.	Raja's Palace	Historical place	65	55
14.	Maa Vairabi Centre	Cultural Organisation	65	48

NARLA BLOCK

Table 4.13 : Arts and Crafts

Arts and crafts/ Place	*Caste of the crafts-man*	*Source of raw material*	*Cost of raw material (Rs.)*	*Market values (Rs. Per Item)*	*Market for selling*	*Distance from District HQ (in km)*	*Public Aware-ness (in percent-age)*
1. Cane work	Dhoba	West Bengal	5000	100-8000	-do-	30	99
2. Bamboo work of Mandel	SC	Lanjigarh Road	Nil	5-200	-do-	46	77
3. Wood works of Mandel	SC	-do-	Nil	200-5000	-do-	46	78
4. Rope making	ST	Local	Nil	10-100	-do-	35	57

Table 4.14 : Natural Resources

Name of Medicinal plants	Usages	Precious stones, etc.
Neem	Multipurpose	Black stone
Babool	-do-	Quartz
Trifala	-do-	Zinc
Duba Grass	-do-	Graphite
Aswagandha	-do-	Mica
—	—	Granite

Table 4.15 : Places of Tourism of Significance

Sl. No.	Name	Tourism Importance	Distance from Dist. HQ (km)	Public awareness (in %)
1.	Asur Gada Fort	Archaeological Spot	35	98
2.	Gada Chandi Temple	Historic/Religious place	34	99
3.	Jaganath Temple	Religious Temple	39	98
4.	Urdani Forest	Wild Life	42	89
5.	Udanti	Picnic Spot	39	85
6.	Sandel	Picnic Spot	35	89
7.	Jonka	Picnic Spot	45	92

THUAMUL RAMPUR BLOCK

Table 4.16 : Arts and Crafts

Arts and crafts/ Place	Caste of the crafts-man	Source of raw material	Cost of raw material (Rs.)	Market values (Rs. Per Item)	Market for selling	Distance from District HQ (in km)	Public Aware-ness (in percent-age)
1. Terra cotta of Balisara	OBC	Local	Nil	10-200	-do-	42	85
2. Brick Making	SC	Local	Nil	800-1000 per thou-sand	-do-	55	88
3. Bamboo basket of Th. Rampur	ST (Kondh)	Local	2-20 per bamboo	30-100	-do-	73	82
4. Khalli making (Leaf Plates)	ST, SC and OBC	Local	Nil	10 per bundle	-do-	73	75

Table 4.17 : Natural Resources

Name of Medicinal plants	*Usages*	*Precious stones*
1. Aswagandha	Multipurpose	Manikya (Diamond)
2. Bramhi	-do-	Kakaneeli
3. Patal garuda	-do-	Biderja
4. Amla	-do-	Catseye
5. Harida	-do-	Gomedha
6. Bahada	-do-	Jabang
7. Kaincha	-do-	Karangdand
8. Bhuin-kakharu	-do-	—
9. Mahua	-do-	—

Table 4.18 : Places of Tourism of Significance

Sl. No.	*Name*	*Tourism Importance*	*Distance from Dist. HQ (km)*	*Public awareness (in %)*
1.	Maharaja Durga Madhava's Palace	Historic Place	73	99
2.	Manikesweri Temple	Religious Place	73	99
3.	Jaganath Temple	Religious Place	72	99
4.	Budharaja Temple	Religious Place	73	99
5.	Nabajiban Organization	Cultural Organization	75	89
6.	Subham Organization	Cultural Organization	75	75
7.	Indrabati and Nagabali Rivers	River Valley Projects	78	95
8.	Hellow/Halo Point	Highest Point from sea level	82	79
9.	Mardiguda	Picnic Spot	73	92
10.	Karlapat	Tiger Sanctuary	73	99
11.	Thakurani Jungle	Wild Life	73	98
12.	Singuri Ghat	Scenic Spot	85	88

Cultural Organisations

The district cultural organization and other voluntary organizations, namely Mahavira Sanskrutika Anushthana and Maharaja P.K. Deo Memorial Ghumra Academy located at Bhawanipatna have been promoting the Ghumra dance of the district. Mr. Jayant Kumar Behera, Mr. Saroj Barik, Mr. Pavitra Gahir and Sudesh Prasad Das are associated with these institutes. They are known as the founder *gurus* of the Ghumra troupes of Kalahandi district. Under their leadership, the Ghumra troupes of the district have participated in various cultural events at various levels such as Block, district, state, national and international levels. The individual contribution of these resource persons particularly towards Ghumra is described as follows :

Resource Persons

- **Mr. Jayant Kumar Behera**

He was the leader of 250 Ghumra artists at ASIAD Games in New Delhi during 1988. The troupes also participated in the Festival of USSR at the international level under his leadership. Further to his credit, the troupes also performed at Fete-de-Pondicherry (State level), Surajkund Mela (Delhi), Konark and Puri Beach festival (State level), Folk dance festival and crafts fair organized by Department of Culture, Government of India on the occasion of the Republic Day, 1993 at New Delhi, ETV programmes at Hyderabad, All India Radio and Doordarshan.

Felicitations :

(a) Felicitated in Silver Jubilee celebrations of Sambalpur University by former Vice President of India, Dr. Shankar Dayal Sharma.
(b) UNICEF award in 1993 by the then Governor of Orissa, Shri Satyanarayana Reddy.
(c) Awarded with cash from "Khariar Sahitya Samiti" of Khariar Block of Kalahandi district.
(d) Felicitated in M.E. Silver Jubilee Celebration.
(e) Awarded by Orissa Sanskrutika Samaj, Sambalpur.

In addition to Ghumra fostering, he has also promoted other folk troupes of Kalahandi district, namely—Madali Folk dance and Banabaadi Folk dance.

• **Mr. Saroj Barik**—His contributions are :

(a) The troupes participated at Inauguration of A.I.R.—1993, Dhenkanal;
(b) Youth festival-1996, Cuttack (district level);
(c) Folk dance festival-1997 and Lok Utsav 2000 at Sambalpur (district level);
(d) Apna Utsav-1989 in Mumbai (State level);
(e) Pondicherry Fete-de—1993 (State level);
(f) West Bengal National Youth Festival (National level);
(g) M.P. Bal Mahotsav-1999 (State level);
(h) ETV programme 2001, AP (State level);
(i) Dweep Mahotsav, 1999, Port Blair (National level);
(j) Shantiniketan festival, 1998 (National level);
(k) New Delhi Utkal Divas, 1998 (National level); and
(l) Sadbhaavana Divas, 1995 at New Delhi (National level).

• **Mr. Pabitra Gahir's Contribution—**

District level :

(a) Inauguration A.I.R.—1993, Dhenkanal;
(b) Cuttack Youth Festival, 1996-98;
(c) Orissa Sangita Natak Academy, Nabrangpur;
(d) Sambalpur Folk Dance Festival, 1997;
(e) Kendrapada—Paradeep Bali Jatra, 1999;
(f) Puri Beach Festival, 1998; and
(g) Cuttack Golden Jubilee function of A.I.R., 1998.

State level :

(a) BBSR-Doordarshan Programme, 1997;
(b) BBSR Republic Day Parade—1997-98;
(c) BBSR Utkal Divas, 1997, 1999;
(d) Karnataka-Orissa Utsav, 2003;
(e) Bihar Kashi Mahotsava, 2002;
(f) Youth Cultural Festival-1998;
(g) Thanjavur—All India Folk Dance Festival and Cultural Fair, 2002;

(h) A.P.—ETV Programme, 2001;
(i) M.P. (Bhopal)—National Tribal Youth Festival, 2000;
(j) West Bengal—Balco Mahotsav, 1999;
(k) A.N. Dweep Mahotsav, 1999; and
(l) Kerala Bharat Utsav, 1994.

National level :

(a) Utkala Divas, Delhi, 1998;
(b) Delhi Trade Fair, 1998; and
(c) Shantiniketan Golden Jubilee Celebration of Indian Independence, 1998.

• **Mr. Sudesh Prasan Dash**—Block Level—Nabrangpur Academy Festival and Sangeet Natak Academy, 1996

District Level :

(a) Bhawanipatna Kalahandi Utsav;
(b) Kendrapada Paradeep Bali Jatra, 1997;
(c) Puri Beach Festival, 1998;
(d) Cuttack Golden Jubilee Function of A.I.R., 1998; and
(e) Anugul Nalco Festival, 2000.

State Level :

(a) MP (Bhopal) National Tribal Youth Festival, 2000;
(b) MP (Korba)—BALCO Mahotsav 1999;
(c) Bihar (Patna) Youth Cultural Festival; and
(d) Pondicherry Fete-de, 1996.

National Level :

(a) Sadbhavana Divas, New Delhi, 1995;
(b) Utkal Divas, 1998; and
(c) Trade Fair, 1998.

• **Maharaja P.K. Deo Memorial Ghumra Academy**—Maharaja Pratap Kesari Deo Ghumra Academy was established in August 1981, in Bhawanipatna with an objective of preservation and promotion of folk dance. Every year 25 to 30 youths undergo training in Ghumra dance in this academy. These dancers have presented their dance in various cultural programmes at the district, State and neighbouring States in collaboration with Mahavir Sanskrutika Anushthana of Bhawanipatna.

Craft Village

There are two Craft Villages, namely Kandagarh Stone Carving Village and Khairiput Wood Carving Village in Koksara and Dharmagarh Blocks respectively. The details of the craft villages are described below :

Stone Carving Village

This village (Photograph 4.3) was established in 1970 by Mr. Gobinda Chandra Majhi, a Kandha tribal man. He is also known as the "master craftsman" and "*guru*" in the area. Mr. Majhi went on a pilgrimage to Lord Jaganath Temple of Puri and Konark Temple with an aim of rediscovering the art of stone carving. His disciple, Mr. Narasingha Naik, a non-tribal man has been strictly following his traditional skills of craftsmanship. Like his *guru,* he also went on a pilgrimage to many historical and tourist sites of Orissa and further developed his skill. Being from an outer locality, he started teaching the village dwellers certain new techniques of craftsmanship in addition to those, which were already prevalent in the area. It is noticed that children between the age group of 4 to 12 are also seen learning the skill from the *guru.* Subsequently, some of the villagers, inspired by him have become his followers and joined him as craftsmen. Their handicrafts such as different animal statues, idols etc. are very popular in the region and have also been acknowledged at national and international levels.

The raw material generally used by them are granite, red stone, which are mostly collected from surrounding local mountains but when they require better quality of raw materials they prefer to get them from other places such as Bhubaneswar, Keonjhar etc.

The craftsmen of this village have participated at various events in Panchayat, Block and district level. Every year, in the month of January under the sponsorship of respective GP, Block and district authority they participate in trade exhibitions. In 2005, they took part in Ekamra Utsav under the sponsorship of Orissa Tourism Department. Even, the tourists from foreign countries such as Australia and Italy had been to their villages and placed huge demands for their handicrafts.

Difficulties that they commonly face are improper marketing of their handicrafts, lack of supply of raw materials and sophisticated instruments for stone carving and absence of any major monetary support from the government.

Khairipadar Wood Carving Centre

The wood carving centre (Photograph 4.6) is located at Khairipadar village at a distance of 10 km away from Dharmagarh Block. Mr. Uddhav Maharana is the founder of this art form. It is learnt from his followers that he started engraving the crafts out of the sandalwoods, which was used as firewood. Gradually, he started selling his wooden art works to earn his livelihood. After his death, his son Mr. Biswamitra Maharana and his brother Mr. Arta Maharana (Photograph 4.5) have been following this traditional skill. Instead of sandalwood, they now use Sal wood as the carving material for the reason that their craft works would not get infested by pests unlike those which were made out of sandalwood.

Due to lack of sal woods in their locality, they purchase wood from Lanjigarh Block. But generally, they try to collect the wood from the local sources under the permission of Bana Sanrakhyana Committee. While collecting the wood from local sources they face many difficulties and are harassed by the forest employees. Although, there is heavy demand of their items but they are not able to fulfil these demands because of lack of wood, financial incentives and modern instruments.

They have participated in various Craft Fairs at Block, district and national levels. In 1997, they took part in Youth

Cultural festivals held in Gujarat, Bihar, Uttar Pradesh and Maharashtra. They also attended New Delhi Trade Fair in 1998 under the sponsorship of Government of Orissa.

Under the initiation of both Mr. Biswamitra Maharana and Mr. Arta Maharana, five SHGs groups have been formed. One amongst these SHGs groups named as Wooden Toy Cooperative Industry Ltd. has been taken into account for the study. The main objective of the group is to generate income through wood craftsmanship and self-sustaining economy. In a group there are 10 to 12 members from the same locality. All the groups have availed the revolving fund provision of Rs. 10,000 per annum and also got the Micro-Credit Finance from SBI, Cooperative Bank and KAGB of Dharmagarh Block. When asked about their mode of credit and loan repayment, it was learnt that they have not faced any problem as their handicrafts are easily sold off at satisfactory market values. At times, they also get demands from other States and abroad as well. They have expressed their gratefulness to Master Craftsman Mr. Arta Maharana who coordinates all the business transactions with respective Government and Non-Governmental agencies for such huge demands of their crafts. The purchasers of their craftworks are both localites and outsiders. There are instances of trips of international tourists from Rome, Soviet Russia and Australia, who purchased their handicrafts paying more than the craftsmen generally expect for their crafts.

It is analyzed from the data that a craftsman on an average Rs. 30,000 to Rs. 40,000, annually gets from the sale of his handicrafts whereas the amount earned by him from other sources are quite less as compared to the sale of his handicrafts. It is observed that craftsmanship is the primary source of sustenance and the other source of income is agriculture (Rs. 10,000 to Rs. 20,000). It is found that the craftsmanship is not only their source of income but also their chief interest. Even though, they independently want to pursue this skill at individual level, they fail to do so as they face financial insecurities and have to undergo more harassment for the procurement of the raw materials. Some of them, who have already invested money individually in this art work are found to be indebted. The craftsmen have been recorded to be under debts of Rs. 2,000 to Rs. 3,000. Since they bring loans from the *sahukar*, they are charged higher interest rates of Rs. 100 to Rs. 200 monthly.

The craftsmen are also sometimes engaged as part-time trainers to train the newly formed group in the district. During this period, they get a consolidated amount of Rs. 1,000 to Rs. 2,000 per month. Further, to upgrade their skill they have to undergo various trainings that are organized at GP, Block, district levels under the supervision of the respective government authority. During the period as a trainer, they get a stipend of Rs. 1,000 to Rs. 2,000 monthly.

Regarding promotion of eco-tourism in the area they are found to be in favour of setting up tourism establishments in their craft villages. Their views are noted as below :

- The wooden craftwork will attract the tourists to their area, which will boost both the tourism and the economic condition of the craftsmen.
- The craftsmanship will be well recognized and adored by the outsiders.

Opinions of Folk Artists

Based on the discussed potential factors, an opinion survey was conducted among the artists, the local businessmen, traders, hoteliers, Government and Non-Government officials with an intention of finding out their views on promoting eco-tourism in their area. It is learnt from the study that the respective troupes have their own views which are recorded as under :

The Ghumra Parties

They are in favour of eco-tourism as according to them :

- Ghumra dance is only limited within Kalahandi district. So also are its instruments. If the domestic or even the foreign tourists will visit their area, the dancers will be glad to entertain them with their folk performances.

- The artists are keen to utilize their folk form as a source of entertainment and also believe that their practices will help in the preservation and spreading of their cultural heritage across.
- By performing, they will also simultaneously earn their livelihood.

Devotional Troupes (Sankirtana Dal)

They intend to perform in front of the tourists to develop a spiritual temperament among their audiences and in return earn self-satisfaction for their job.

Folk Drama and Song

According to their perception, if tourism will be promoted in their region, there will be enhancement of their art forms and culture on the whole.

Dhap Parties

They have expressed their positive attitude towards promoting eco-tourism as they believe :

- Both the dance and the instruments (Dhap) will definitely attract the tourists.
- The income of the artists will grow eventually.

Kureiphula and Ghadel

The dancers of these troupes favoured the setting up of eco-tourism in their regions as they feel that at least through this system, they might get acknowledged by the people and be recognized and sought by the District Cultural Organisations.

Opinions of Elite Group/Stakeholders

This group includes government officials, politicians, businessmen, travel agencies, traders and hoteliers. An opinion survey was conducted to know about the general awareness on tourism potentialities of the area. It is learnt that :

- The district is full of hill and mountain ranges and natural scenic beauty.
- The people are simple, honest and welcoming.
- It has its regional dialect with a soothing accent.
- Ethnic food and beverages offered in these regions are worth mentioning.
- Nua Khai festival and Chatar Jatra of Dusehra are famous festivals.
- The district is well connected with other parts of the State through road and airways.

Possible Impact of Tourism

After analyzing the empirical data, in the people's view with regard to possible impact of eco-tourism in their area, it is found that the people have mentioned both positive and negative effects of the tourism which are mentioned as below :

Possible Positive Impact

- Flourishing of trade business.
- Development of marketing facilities for local produces.
- Wide publicity of local art and folk culture.
- Employment opportunities for local unemployed people.
- Facilitation of better infrastructure development such as road, electricity, health care facilities, etc.
- Special status or identity to that particular area, which in the long run will lead towards prosperity.

Possible Negative Impact

- Environment will be polluted.
- Price hike of the essential commodities due to inflow of visitors and tourism.
- Possibility of outbreak of foreign epidemical diseases.

- Presence of anti-social elements and their organizations
- Criminal activities such as theft and robbery might increase.
- Outsiders may face problems interacting with the local people and it might lead to language and class dispute in the locality.

Proposed Model Tourist Villages and Eco-Tourism Centre

Focus Group Discussion (FGD) was adopted to find out the proposed Eco-tourism Centre and tourist villages. The method and the questions which were employed are mentioned as under :

Method

- 10 to 20 interested participants were invited.
- Participant's age, educational status, awarcness of eco-tourism concept, participation at the district cultural events, were taken into account.
- The venues were selected in advance. For this the youth club centre, troupe's training place, craft centre and school, were used.

Questions

- Have you ever participated in such type of gathering ?
- Have you ever witnessed the folk dance of Kalahandi ? Please tell some of them.
- Name some tourist spots of your locality.
- Do you think that your place is ideal for promoting eco-tourism ?
- Which block of Kalahandi district will be suitable for Eco-tourism Centre and why ?

PRA method was adopted to find out the people views on the establishment of eco-tourism centre and model tourist villages in the study Blocks. The entire process involved the active participation of the public. The findings were interpreted, discussed and recorded according to the people's perspective towards the whole conception of eco-tourism. The said method was incorporated as under :

- 10 to 20 persons who were folk troupes, artisans, villagers, teachers and ward members.
- Paper, pen and pencils were provided.
- Participants were told to draw a sketch of tourist map of their locality indicating the distance from the district headquarters, location of tourist place and folk troupe's habitats.
- Utmost care was taken to encourage the voluntary participation of the individual participant in the process.

Highlights of Findings

Majority of choices regarding the Eco-Tourism centre (Fig. 4.1) goes in favour of Bhawanipatna for its proper connectivity to proposed tourist villages and other districts (Fig. 4.2). The reasons are discussed below :

- District Headquarters and prevailing communication facilities such as road, rail and train connectivity.
- It will provide all the necessary administrative support to the domestic and international tourists.
- The tourists will be able to approach the Block by Kesinga Railway Station, by road or by air as shown in Fig. 4.2.
- A Museum displaying tribal and local artifacts and handicrafts.
- A centre for the tourists to shop local arts and crafts.
- A herbal medication centre.

Operational Modalities of the Tourism Centre

For the resting purposes of the tourists, accommodation facilities in the forms of cottages, rest houses should be constructed by government and public partnership. These

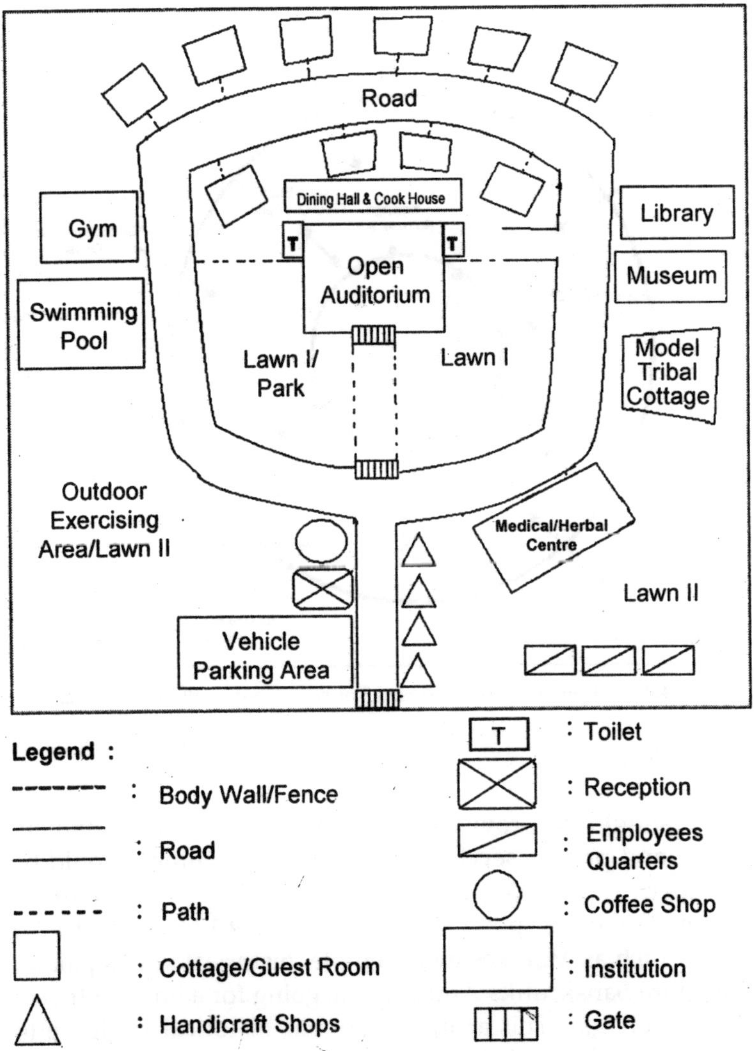

Fig. 4.1 : Design of Proposed Tourism Centre/Village

constructions should be made inside a separate tourist complex with security provisions so that the tourists having reached Bhawanipatna will be able to take rest comfortably. They may chalk out their trips to visit the surrounding areas/Blocks of the district within a short span of visit.

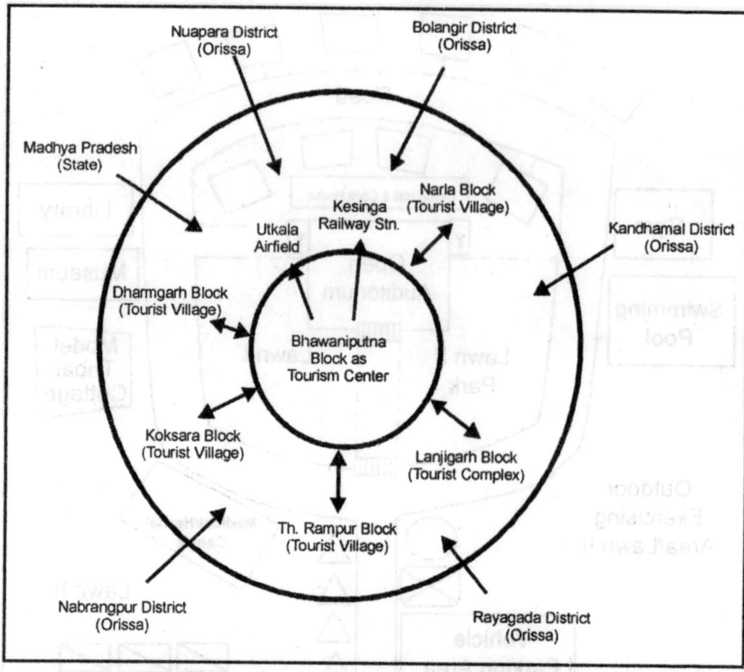

Fig 4.2 : Connectivity to Proposed Tourism Centre (Bhawanipatna)

Travel Plan

There should be provisions of proper conveyances, namely OTDC and private services. Besides, food facilities should be provided. A suitable plan for the tourists start their tour by visiting the scenic spots (Photographs 4.12, 4.13, 4.14, and 4.21) places such as Manikeshwari temple, historical king's palace, Mahavira Sanskrutika Anushthana, going for a boating trip in the Asha Sagar. This artificial lake has historical evidence to its origin. Maharaja Udit Pratap Deo of Kalahandi dynasty had dug this lake near Arkabaali Mountain (Arkabaali Dongar) and named it 'Asha Sagar' after his queen's (Rani's) name 'Asha Kumari'. Till date the beautiful lake is used and adored by the public. They may come back to the tourism centre at the end of the day. In the evening, the tourists should be enabled to enjoy Ghumra folk dance and music in the Centre itself, buy

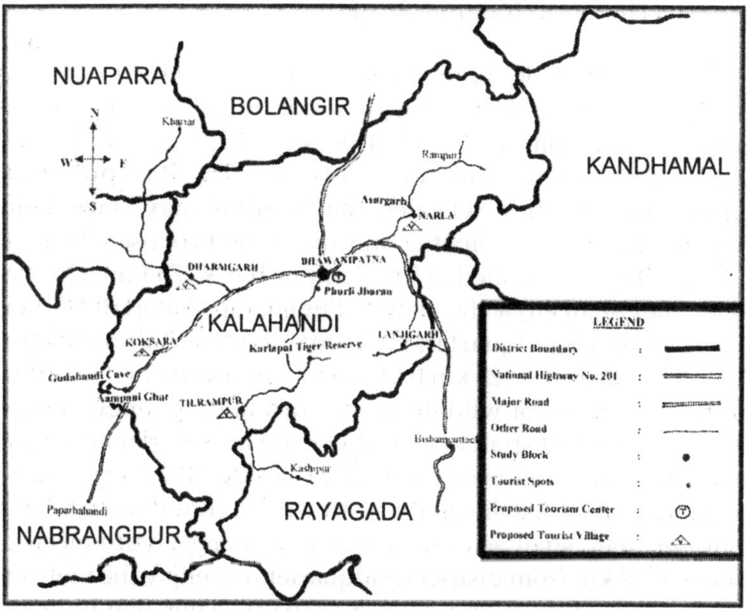

Map 4.1 : Proposed Tourist Villages in Kalahandi District

ethnic handicrafts from stalls in the Centre, have their dinner constituting of ethnic food and beverages, and finally go to rest for the day in their cottages or guest houses. Next day morning, the tourist may proceed towards the Tourist villages. These tourist villages should be set up in other Blocks. According to the people's perception, in every Tourist Village there should be provision of cottages, ethnic food and beverages, handicraft centres, museums, entertainment shows, herbal/health care centre, hiking and trekking facilities to the scenic spots, tribal habitats and Craft Villages.

Model Tourist Villages

It is observed that the people of the study Blocks have given their own suggestions regarding the settlement of Model Tourist Villages (Map 4.1).

A. Th. (Thuamul) Rampur Block

The people of Th. Rampur Block have expressed their views in PRA (Photograph 4.28) through a road map showing tourist sites (Photographs 4.17, 4.18, 4.19, 4.20, 4.22, 4.23, 4.24, 4.25 and 4.26) astride the road between Th. Rampur and Bhawanipatna. It is revealed that tourists may start their journey from Bhawanipatna and reach the proposed Tourist Village (Fig. 4.3) located in Th. Rampur Block (73 km). On the way, they shall enjoy the view of Phuljharan Waterfall (15 km from district headquarters) and may have a halt at Jakam Wooden Bungalow (25 km from district headquarters) in order to have a glance of wildlife of the surrounding jungle. From there, they might straightaway move towards Karlapatta tiger sanctuary and shall enjoy the wildlife. Besides, they might have a glance of the tribal life in the nearby tribal (Kandha) habitats. Further, they shall advance towards Kunang Hydro-electric project (78 km from district headquarters) to enjoy the view of river valley project and river Nagabadi. After one hour of journey, they shall reach at road side village Balisara (42 km from the district headquarters). Here, the tourists will witness the local pottery and terra cotta skills and works at the workshops. At the same place, they may have an observation of local weekly market (Photograph 4.23), bamboo handicrafts, khapar and brick making skills of the local people. At the end of the day, they shall reach their final destination of the Tourist Village at Th. Rampur. They shall have a night stay in the cottages with an ethnic dinner, entertainment by folk dances (Dhap, Salap Nisan and Ghumra). Next day morning, the tourists will move forward to Manikeshwari Temple, kings's palace and Lord Jaganath temple. Then the tourists may proceed towards Singhari Ghati (the zig-zag curving path) and Mardiguda (the place of origin of Indrabati river) which are both located within a distance of 3-4 km from Th. Rampur. After visiting the Ghati, they may take a detour to the opposite direction climbing Hallow Point (8 to 10 km from Th. Rampur), the highest point from the sea shore in Orissa. Then they shall come back to the cottages, have their lunch and on the same day may return back to Bhawanipatna Tourism Centre.

B. Dharmagarh Block

The people have proposed to set up a Tourist Village at Khairipadar wood craft Village (45 km from the District headquarters). This carving centre has a wider reputation and popularity in the district. Besides wood carving craftsmanship, the Block has nine folk troupes belonging to different categories, namely devotional folk drama, folk musical groups and Ghumra dance. On the way from Bhawanipatna to Craft Village, they shall come across Junagarh Block and witness the weaving skill of *saree* at Chichiguda Weaving Centre. Besides, they may have a glimpse of archaeological monuments and famous Budhist Temple at Lankeshwari. Before touching craft village, they may visit to Paradeshwara Temple of Lord Shiva (Photographs 4.7 and 4.8) in the outskirts of the Block. The temple is named after Shiva Linga which is made of mercury (*parada*). Water channels of Indrabati Hydo-electricity project also surround the area and it is really a worth watching site. It will take about half an hour for the tourists to reach the craft village from the Block headquarters. On the way to the craft village, they may enjoy the surrounding green fields. At the craft village, they may have their lunch and witness the woodcrafts at the workshops and may also buy the crafts. They may stay in the cottages for the night while relishing upon ethnic food and colourful folk dance. They might also visit the weekly market (Photograph 4.9). Next day morning, they may plan towards Koksara Block or go back to the Tourism Centre (Bhawanipatna).

C. Koksara Block

The participants of Focus Group Discussion (FGD) (Photograph 4.27) of the Block suggested Kandagarh Stone Carving Village (Photograph 4.3) as Model Tourist Village of the Block (Map 4.1). It is observed that the Block is suitable for enhancing eco-tourism through tourism avenues and the Kandagarh Stone Carving Village as it is treated as one of the most resourceful area for promoting eco-tourism.

Koksara is a road side Block next to NH 201 which leads towards Nabrangpur district, situated at a distance of 85 km away from the district headquarters. From the Tourism Centre towards Koksara, the tourists can enjoy greenery of agricultural fields on the way. After reaching at Koksara, they may move towards Aampani, a Ghat village which is located beside the State Highway that leads towards Koraput district. Ampani is a hilly village surrounded by the dense forests rich in flora and fauna, namely sal, teak, karuma trees and deer, wild boars etc. The visitors, 4 to 5 km ahead from this place may proceed towards Gudahandi and Dokrichanchari to see Prehistoric Caves and paintings on its wall. One can take a left turn towards Kasana Hill, a scenic spot and also enjoy Maadali folk dance at Supad village. The tourists can also take a detour to the right direction and reach Karak Waterfall (5 km from Aampani) and simultaneously enjoy the folk dance of Kureiphula troupe and Ghadel troupe. The tourists should then come back to Aampani and move towards the Model tourist village of Kandagarh stone craft village to take shelter. During their night stay, they may enjoy the folk dance, ethnic food and beverages and shop herbal medicines and stone crafts from the local artisans. In the morning, the tourists may start for nearby Budharaja Temple (Photograph 4.4) that has a historical significance. Budharaja, the King of Bhawanipatna, built the temple. Legend says that Budharaja was a famous warrior and the people observe festivals like Dusehra, sacrificing goats in his remembrance till this date. The tourists shall witness the stone carving skills of the craftsmen. After their lunch, they may come back to the Tourism Centre (proposed) at Bhawanipatna.

D. Narla Block

The participants of Focus Group Discussion unanimously express their views for a Model Tourist Village at Asurgarh village. They also proposed a Museum to be built inside the premises of Asurgarh Fort (Photographs 4.1 and 4.2) at Asurgarh village (35 km from district headquarters). At the

Narla Road Junction, they will witness the cane work (Photographs 4.10 and 4.11) and take a right turn to reach Madel Bamboo Woodcraft Centre (46 km from the District Headquarters). Then they might visit the Jaganath Temple within the Narla township and may move towards Asurgarh Fort. They may have their lunch and take rest for one hour in the cottages in the Model Tourist Village. In the afternoon, they may approach Gadachandi Temple located at the entrance of the Fort. The temple is famous for Goddess Chandi and statue of Kalapahaad (Photograph 4.2). There is a legendary tale about the authenticity of the temple. It says that Kalapahaad who was a Muslim soldier got married to a Hindu girl and became motivated towards Hinduism and established this temple in the honour of Goddess Chandi. The visitors may have a bird's eye view of the square shaped Fort. From both the archaeological and historical point of view, the Fort has a great significance in the modern era. From archaeological evidences, the Fort dates back to 3000 AD to 5000 AD and was known as the capital city of Maharaja Gosingh dynasty. The archaeological findings of this place also gives proof of the presence of a Mint House. All those findings after excavation have been taken and preserved at the State Museum Bhawanipatna and the process is still going on.

The people of the area have expressed their dissatisfaction regarding the preservation of monuments at the State Museum Bhubaneswar. According to them, they have all the rights over the monuments excavated from their place as they feel it is their ancestral heritage. They suggest that the government should open a museum within the premises of the Fort with a view to preserving these monuments in the place where they belong. Further, the people complained about poor connectivity to the Fort and expressed their desire to have a proper road to the Fort.

During the night stay, tourists may enjoy the ethnic food and entertainment show of folk drama and colourful Ghumra dance. On the next day morning, they may either go back to the Tourism Centre (Bhawanipatna) or proceed towards Lanjigarh Block as the Lanjigarh Block lies close to Narla Block.

E. Lanjigarh Block

People actively took part in the Focus Group Discussion. They were of the opinion that a Tourist Rest House should be constructed at Bishwanathpur, which is the Block headquarters. Regarding the tourist plan, they have mentioned their views as below :

The tourists on the way from Narla to Lanjigarh Block may enjoy the scenic forest view. After reaching the Block, they may began their trip from the Kutia Kandha Development Agency (KKD) which has been working for the integrated development of the Kutia Kandha PTGs of Orissa. The Microproject (KKD) will provide them necessary information about PTG and their habitats. After that, they may move towards Vedanta Alumina Ltd. Company (Photograph 4.15) to have a glance of the establishment. Their visit will be more enjoyable if they shall visit the Niyamgiri Hill Range, which is the habitat of Kutia Kandha and Dongria Kandha people and also the treasure house of herbal medicines and wildlife. Next day morning, they may plan to visit other tourist places, namely Old Palace (Photograph 4.16), Kidingi Mountain Range, Kadali Ghat, Bansadharaa river, Ret River and Sikurkuppa Ghat. They might cover these places while returning back to the Tourism Centre (Bhawanipatna).

PHOTOGRAPHS

Photograph 4.1 : Asurgarh Fort behind the cliff in Narla Block

Photograph 4.2 : Statue of Kalapahaada (Centre) at the Temple at Asurgarh Fort, Narla

Photograph 4.3 : Stone Carving Centre at Craft Village of Kandagarh, Koksara Block

Photograph 4.4 : Budharaja Temple of Aampani GP, Koksara Block

Photograph 4.5 : Master Craftsman Mr. Arta Maharana of Wood Craft Village, Khairipadar of Dharmagarh Block

Photograph 4.6 : Wood Crafts displayed at Wood Craft Centre of Khairipadar, Dharmagarh Block

Photograph 4.7 : Paradeshwar Temple at Dharmagarh

Photograph 4.8 : Shiv Linga made of Mercury (*Parad*) at Paradeshwar Temple, Dharmagarh Block

Photograph 4.9 : Weekly Market at Dharmagarh Block

Photograph 4.10 : Cane furniture works of Cane Centre, Narla Block

Photograph 4.11 : Cane Centre of Narla Block

Photograph 4.12 : Maharaja Palace at Bhawanipatna

Photograph 4.13 : Darbaar Hall in front of the Maharaja Palace, Bhawanipatna

Photograph 4.14 : Bhawanishankar Temple of Bhawanipatna

Photograph 4.15 : Vedanta Alumina Ltd., Lanjigarh

Photograph 4.16 : Old Palace of Lanjigarh

Photograph 4.17 : Origin of Indrabati River at Mardiguda, Th. Rampur Block

Photograph 4.18 : Indrabati River, Th. Rampur Block

Photograph 4.19 : Hydro-electric power Chamber in Kuang, Th. Rampur Block

Photograph 4.20 : Manikeshwari Temple at Th. Rampur

Photograph 4.21 : Phurlijharan Waterfall at Bhawanipatna

Photograph 4.22 : Terra Cotta and Khappar Making Centre at Balisara, Th. Rampur Block

Photograph 4.23 : Weekly Market in Saisuruni, Th. Rampur Block

Photograph 4.24 : Unused Tourist Building, Th. Rampur Block

Photograph 4.25 : Revenue Bungalow, Th. Rampur

Photograph 4.26 : King's Palace, Th. Rampur

Photograph 4.27 : Focus Group Discussion at Koksara

Photograph 4.28 : Participants of PRA, Th. Rampur

5

Summary and Policy Recommendations

The present study has tried to find out the role of folk dance and music in promoting eco-tourism in Kalahandi district of Orissa. Besides, it has also tried to identify the other tourism potential factors of the district for facilitating eco-tourism in the region. It has eight objectives which have guided the entire process of data collection and analysis. The findings of the study have been incorporated in four chapters. The analysis of the data has been made according to the sample folk troupes in six study Blocks.

Major Findings

The KBK region is one of the most backward regions in the State. Poor road connectivity is one of the important facet of its backwardness. The district Kalahandi is one among the KBK districts. The Biju KBK plan for the eight KBK districts under the State plan gives emphasis—(a) creating opportunities for economic, social and human development for the people in the region; (b) accelerating poverty reduction and achieving millennium development goal; and (c) improving the quality of life of the local people and bringing the region at par with other developed region under Special Connective Programme (SCP). The plan further highlights about the all weather connectivity of the villages to habitations with a minimum population between 250 to 500. The State Government under its tourism policy has decided to upgrade and repair 269 roads to improve communication facilities to different tourists places of Orissa.

According to National Council of Applied Economic Research (NCAER), total contribution of tourism to both direct and indirect employment is estimated at over 8.5 per cent. If the National Sample Survey (NSS) results on employment and unemployment are taken into account, in Orissa employment opportunities in the tourism characteristic goods and services like hotels, food and beverage services, have risen by a whopping 15 per cent (*The New Indian Express* : September 28, 2007). It also states that all these means of tourism promotion policies and growth of the related sector, could do wonders for the State. For this Orissa must redefine tourism. But in order to tap the employment potential the State needs to augment tourist infrastructure. Till date State has mere 1 per cent share in domestic tourist traffic. On the other hand, it shares only 0.9 per cent in foreign tourist traffic. State's vulnerability to adverse climatic phenomenon and health profile, e.g. cyclone, epidemics etc. are working as deterrent factors for attracting the tourist flow. In 2006, Orissa received 52 lakh domestic and 39 thousand foreign tourists. During their average four-day stint here, each domestic tourist spent Rs. 7,100 and a foreign tourist shelled out Rs. 26,000 during the thirteen-day stay.

The Assembly Committee on tourism has recommended the State Government to promote rural tourism to generate employment opportunities. The Committee directed the tourism department to identify places viable for rural tourism and start necessary work for development of such sites to attract tourists. Further stating that eco-tourism has immense potential for growth, the panel suggested that the Department of Forest and Environment should allow Department of Tourism to implement eco-tourism project in the forest areas. The Committee also recommended that a Budget provision for conservation of 218 protected monuments in the State, should be increased. There are 218 protected monuments under the Department of Culture and 79 more under Archaeological Survey of India. However, more than 3,000 temples and unprotected monuments remain unattended.

On account of eco-tourism projects in the State, there has been a provision of Central Government's assistance of Rs. 50 crore for the maintenance of an Eco-Tourism Centre and an Eco-Tourist Circuit. In the current year (2008), the State has received a Budgetary allocation of rupees five crore from the Central Government for the development of five Eco-Tourism Centres and rupees eight crore towards two Circuits (*The Samaja* : January 2008). However, according to the Department of Orissa Tourism, the funds should be properly utilized.

Despite being richly gifted by nature, the virgin tourist destinations of Western Orissa remain unexplored. Tourism in the region remains a non-starter even though it has the potential to generate self-employment both direct and indirect and boost the region's economy. The world's longest earthen Hirakud Dam, scope of water sports, trekking, historical tourism and wildlife, scope of tribal tourism, religious places, folk dance and music are all here but due to lack of Government support to promote the same has left the region to struggle for recognition. The Gandhamardhan Hill range (Sambalpur district) and Niyamgiri Hill (Kalahandi district) are the treasure house of herbal medicines. The temples in Sonpur, Bolangir, Nuapada and Kalahandi districts are archaeological wonders. Nuapada is famous for its 64 Yogini Temples of Shakti culture.

The region is equally famous for folk dance and songs which are blend of love, romance, satire, teasing, and many sweet thoughts. The most popular folk songs and dance of Western Orissa are—Dalkhai, Rasarkeli, Nachnia, Dhap, Ghumra, etc. In the same spirit various cultural functions like Kalahandi Mahotsav, Bedavyaas Nrutyotsav, Sambalpur Loka Mahotsava and Pradhanpat Festival, are being organized at the respective GP, Block and District level.

Kalahandi is a hidden paradise for tourists for its unparallel natural beauty. It has unlimited potential not only in the sphere of eco-tourism, but also for ethno-tourism, religious tourism and cultural tourism. The present study provides the empirical evidences (six study Blocks) of these tourism factors along with the potentialities of folk dance and music for boosting eco-tourism in the region. At the same time necessary suggestion/policy recommendations are also given.

Folk Dance and Artists

In the district a total number of 52 Folk troupes have been identified from six Blocks constituting 21 GPs (Table 2.1). They have been divided into four categories, namely Ghumra, Devotional, Folk drama; and Tribal folk dance troupes. It has been found that the Ghumra dance is the most well known dance form of the district and has earned laurels at various levels, namely, GP, Block, State, National and International levels (Table 2.4). The next popular form of folk dance is "Dhap" which is basically a tribal dance and found in the tribal dominated Blocks of Th. Rampur and Lanjigarh. The Folk drama and Sankirtan parties have the popularities only in the respective Blocks and the regions.

Each troupe has its own core identity in its theme, costumes, instruments and practice form. It is observed that majority of instruments and costumes are brought from Junagarh Block whereas modern instruments and attires are purchased from Raipur (Chhattisgarh State). The maintenance as well as purchase of costumes and instruments, are done with member's contributions. It has been recorded that for the sustenance of their dance activities they do not get any financial benefit from other source (Government/NGOs).

In regard to their participation, out of 52 troupes, it is found that almost all have participated in GP and Block level. However, only 36 groups have been participated in district level. Among them only 10 troupes have taken part in State level whereas only six troupes got the opportunity to perform at the national level. There are only two Ghumra troupes, taken part in the international competition. It is observed that Ghumra is the only troupe which has represented in both at the national and international level (Table 2.4).

It is learnt from the opinion survey that all the troupes are in favour of eco-tourism in their area as according to them their dance forms will be well recognized as well as they will earn better remuneration from the tourists. However, they have stated their expectations which are as mentioned below :

- Financial support;
- Hope for modern instruments;
- Club house for training;
- New story line;
- Good infrastructure (road, water, electricity facilities);
- Patronization of troupes at cultural festivals organized at all levels (GP, Block, State, national and international) and they should be well informed in advance before the scheduled events;
- For outside organized events they should be provided with proper food, accommodation and conveyance; and
- During the participations in the cultural events, they should be allowed to perform in their own traditional attires but not according to the respective event organizer.

Dying Folk Troupes

It is learnt from the empirical evidences that certain folk dances are found to be in dying state. Block-wise details of these troupes along with the reasons are mentioned below :

A. Bhawanipatna Block—Five troupes, namely Kitchakabadh folk drama, Hirabatiharana, Subhadraharan, Gangadevi Natak Dala, and Lankapodi and Sitaharan, are no more in practice form. The main reason is learnt that the younger generation is no more interested in these mythological dramas. On the other hand older generations are no more alive to teach the younger generations.
B. Dharmagarh Block—Two troupes, namely Nagapada Arjuna Nataka Dal and Maa Manikeswari Dal are in dying state. It is learnt that the former troupe became disintegrated because of intra-conflicts in the troupe and the later was broken because of discouragement and financial support.

C. Lanjigarh Block—Four folk troupes, namely Patrapada Sankirtana Dal, Pujaripada Natak Party, Agni Bhairabi Natak Party and Solaboida are not in practice. The reasons which are found to be associated are—Misunderstanding among the members, lack of time, disinterest attitudes of youngsters, and death of the artists.

D. Th. Rampur Block—One troupe, namely Khanduan Party broke because of intra-rivalry among its members.

Musical Instruments not in use

Similarly, certain traditional instruments are no more found to be in used state. Details of these instruments along with the reasons, are given below :

- Crunch (*sankha*)—Non-availability.
- Singh Baja—It is a large sized instrument of a single membrane drum to which two thorns are attached. Two artists have to play the instruments simultaneously in which danger involves. Because of the risk factor the Government has banned it.
- Khanjani—Lack of availability of Iguana skin for membrane of Drum.
- Maadal—Because of non-availability of monkey skin for membrane of Drum.
- Timtin—Lack of appreciation from the audience.
- Dhola—The performers found it difficult to coordinate its sound with other musical instruments.

Findings of Socio-economic Conditions

Major findings on their socio-economic profile are described as under :

Age-wise Distribution

It is found that out of 52 sample troupes constituting 686 members, 67 are under the age group of 10 to 17 years, which accounts 9.77 per cent of the total members (Table 3.1). On the other hand there are 286 members (41.69%) within the age group of 18 to 25 years of the troupe members. There are higher accounts of the elderly members (26-31 and 32-50), who constitute 25.22 per cent and 20.6 per cent respectively.

This, however, gives a different picture if we consider individual Block status. Bhawanipatna Block shares the same status as of the overall district pattern. The Dharmagada Block depicts 37.78 per cent members belonging within the age groups of 32 to 50 and above. On the other hand Koksara and Lanjigarh project a different age group profile in which 8.57 per cent and 7.2 per cent members are under the age group bracket of 32 to 50. It also indicates the inclination of more percentage (21 and 18) of younger people towards folk dance. The rest two Blocks, namely Narla and Th. Rampur also presents the maximum percentage (46.55 and 50.9) of younger people in the troupes.

Marital Status

There is a definite impact of marital status both on the performance level and economic aspect of the folk troupes. The overall marital status (Table 3.1) reveals that a majority of membership accounts for married members which constitute 80.61 per cent in comparison to unmarried members of 19.39 per cent. However, an inclination of unmarried younger mass towards their respective folk practices is also witnessed in troupes of Bhawanipatna, Koksara, Lanjigarh and Th. Rampur. But to the exception, Dharmagarh and Narla illustrates the presence of only married members in the troupes.

Educational Status

Only 23.03 per cent (Table 3.2) members are illiterate out of 686 members in the district. On the other hand, a majority of members (70.24%) share a higher status in the formal education achievement. This shows that irrespective of the educational status, the folk population of the district continues to have an inclination towards their respective folk dance and music. Except Lanjigarh Block, there are 3.49 per cent members, who have attained secondary education.

Occupational Status

It is observed that a major portion of 51.31 per cent (Table 3.3) is dependent on daily wages whereas 24.19 per cent are engaged in agricultural sector. Out of 686 troupe artists, 14.87 per cent are skilled labourers, only 3.49 per cent in government sector and only 3.49 per cent in business. However, the troupe members of Lanjigarh Block show a different occupational status with 95 per cent members busy in skilled and daily wage labourers. There is a student in the troupe also.

Economic Status

The economic status (Table 3.4) of a folk artist of the Narla Block is the highest among all the troupes, which constitutes a major share of possession of landed property (82.57%), livestock (7.46%). Again with troupe's assets, the Block shows higher share (2.83%). It is followed by Bhawanipatna Block (Rs. 85,583.60), which constitutes 80.77 per cent of landed property and household utensils (11.94 %). On the other hand, the net economic status of a Lanjigarh folk artist is quite poor (Rs. 35,493.36) in the district. However, from the overall economic status it has been observed that a folk artist of Kalahandi district possesses 82.86 per cent of landed property, 14.62 per cent of household assets and 2.51 per cent of troupe's assets out of his total economic strength in average.

Annual Income

The annual household income of a folk artist has been calculated taking into account the income raised from the major livelihood sources and folk dance. The average annual income of a folk artist of Bhawanipatna Block is recorded as the highest (Rs. 26,725.7). The net income accounts to 5.51 per cent share to folk dance, 5.63 per cent to Minor Forest Produces (MFP) and 47.52 per cent to agriculture/horticulture produces (Table 3.5). The folk artist of Narla Block has the second highest income (Rs. 22,731.25). Among all the folk artists, Koksara Block performers indicate the lowest annual income (Rs. 16,921.31) followed by Dharmagarh Block (Rs. 17,717.4) and Th. Rampur (Rs. 19,260). On an average, a folk artist of Kalahandi district annually earns Rs. 20,745.74 from various sources of which folk dance accounts 4.55 per cent that is almost equal to MFP income (5.35%).

Annual Expenditure

It is observed that higher the income level, lower is the percentage of income spent on food items. Based on NSS's per capita monthly consumer expenditure, the annual expenditure of the troupes have been calculated. Bhawanipatna Block states the highest annual expenditure (Rs. 39,979) with 55.39 per cent spent on food items and 44.61 per cent on non-food items (Table 3.6). While Lanjigarh Block accounts the lowest (Rs. 21,790) annual expenditure. Overall, the same ratio of expenditure on food and non-food items is seen in rest of the Blocks. This indicates that the folk artists of all the six study Blocks fall within the category of BPL status. However, it is learnt from the income and expenditure comparison that all the folk artists have somehow managed within a deficit Budget.

Regarding savings and indebtedness (Table 3.7), it has been found that the average annual indebtedness (Rs. 1,608.38) is more than the average annual savings (Rs. 472.17).

Health Care Provisions

The diseases which are commonly prevalent are malaria, jaundice, diarrhoea and skin diseases. People apply both the tradition/herbal and modern health care facilities. The only problem faced by them is the lack of primary health centres and hospitals for which they generally depend on the PHC located in the Block and district headquarters. Generally, the people of these areas depend on Government hospital of Bhawanipatna as it is the only hospital which provides adequate health care facilities.

Eco-tourism in general connotation means about management of local resources—Human and Natural. From the evidential findings, it has been recorded that besides having 52 types of folk troupes, the district with its twenty types of arts and craft works (Tables 4.1, 4.4, 4.7, 4.10, 4.13 and 4.16) do justify its name as "Kalahandi" or "Pots of Arts". Apart from these, there are other boosting natural sources (Tables 4.2, 4.5, 4.8, 4.11, 4.14 and 4.17) such as abundances of herbal medicines (55 types), mineral resources (34 types), and 76 tourist places are also found to be present (Tables 4.3, 4.6, 4.9, 4.12, 4.15 and 4.18).

It is learnt from the findings of the opinion survey, FD and PRA method that majority of the troupes members have given their positive opinions on the eco-tourism. Simultaneously, they have also mentioned about the negative aspect of eco-tourism in their regions. In regard to positive impact, the artists are in the opinion that eco-tourism will certainly enhance their economic conditions through tourists flow to their areas. While stating about the negativity, there is an apprehension that there might be risk of pollution and other health hazards, namely AIDS, malaria, gastrointestinal and other contaminated diseases throughout side visitors.

The findings of PRA and FD, highlights the importance of two prominent handicraft centres, namely, Stone Carving Centre (Kandagarh village) and Wood Craft Works (Khairiput village) for facilitation of eco-tourism activities in the district. Furthermore, it has been noted that craftsmanship is the primary economic source as a craftsman on an average gets Rs. 30,000 to Rs. 40,000 annually. It is learnt that they face difficulties in procuring the raw materials and are found to be in an indebted state. Regarding promotion of eco-tourism, they are found to be in favour of setting up tourism establishments in their craft villages.

In regard to proposed Model Tourist Village and Eco-Tourism Centre, it is found that people have the opinion of developing an Eco-Tourism Centre at Bhawanipatna and the Model Tourist Villages at the other five Blocks. According to them model tourists villages should come up in these Blocks in a suitable locality. Moreover, Bhawanipatna being the district headquarters and with all administrative facilities, it will easily facilitate coordination with other Blocks through the respective model tourist villages (Fig. 4.1, Map 4.1).

Policy Recommendations

The empirical findings about the folk artists and viable tourism factors, analysed from the perspective of eco-tourism in the district, led further to policy recommendation which are enumerated below :

- All the folk troupes of the district should get equal patronization in respect of promotion of their dance forms.
- State level conference should be organized in collaboration with Ministry of Culture to popularize the folk dance and music of Kalahandi district.
- Folk artists feel neglected, according to them they are not given due weightage to participate in Kalahandi Mahotsava (district level) and also in other cultural events. Instead of them, the college students are invited to participate in these organized programmes. Generally, these students perform the folk dance with wrong costumes and jewelleries, which the traditional folk artists seem to be upset about. The artists feel that such careless attitude towards the ethnicity of the folk dance forms tends to create a bad or false image to the original identity of the dance forms. So, these artists should get proper patronization from the respected cultural authority at all levels.
- Folk dances of this region are on the verge of extinction. The reasons may be with the advent of television and films which have led to its dwindling popularity. The younger generations are found to be not keen in folk

practice. Efforts should be made by NGOs, private cultural organizations and the District Cultural Organization to revive these dance forms.

- The State Government may engage these folk artists in mass awareness programmes, namely RTI, AIDS, Maleria, Pulse Polio, Literacy campaign, Safe drinking water, Sanitation etc.
- As regard to the economic conditions, necessary steps should be taken to provide 100 days employment to the folk artists under NREGS (National Rural Employment Guarantee Scheme) as they are yet to get the benefit.
- Necessary supports of financial and raw materials should be provided to the craftsmen of the district. Besides, proper marketing infrastructure should be provided.
- At Bhawanipatna, a Tourism Centre must be established with a proper tourism complex and necessary infrastructures. The Tourism complex should constitute cottages, rest houses, museum, handicraft centre, herbal medical care centres, proper arrangements for food and beverages and provision for the folk artists and dancers to perform and entertain the tourists. Local people should be engaged as guides, hoteliers and for travelling purposes.
- Airfield located at Utkela which is about 20 km away from the district headquarters should be made into operational to facilitate both the domestic and international tourists.
- Under Comprehensive Heritage Policy of the Government necessary steps should be taken to protect the archaeological monuments and temples of the district by the Cultural Department and Archaeological Survey of India.
- Adequate steps should be taken by the Government to renovate the abandoned and dilapidated tourist complexes which are located at Th. Rampur, Dharmagarh, and Bhawanipatna. The artificial lake

"Asha Sagar" of Bhawanipatna, may be beautified with facilities of boating, rowing, and angling.

- Steps may be taken by the Orissa Tourism Department to set up Model tourist villages at the proposed sites of the other five Blocks.
- Forest and Environment Department may allow Orissa Tourism Department to implement eco-tourism project in the forest areas. Under this, eco-clubs may be established in these locality with public support.
- The Orissa Tourism Department may consider these identified tourist viable resources of the Kalahandi district for boosting eco-tourism.

Implications of the Study

I hope the findings of the report will be useful to the Ministry of Tourism/HRD (Human Resource Development), Government of India, policy-makers, researchers, NGOs, and academics who have passion for research in this area. It will also help the planners and policy-makers in deciding appropriate policy/interventions to improve socio-economic conditions of the people through promotion of eco-tourism in the district.

Bibliography

Behura, N.K. and N. Panigrahi (2001). *Functioning of the Fifth Schedule of the Constitution in the State of Orissa.* Bhubaneswar : N.K.C.D.S.

Bhatta, S.C. and Gopal K. Bhargava (2005). *Land and People of Indian States and Union Territories : Chhattisgarh.* Volume 6, pp. 243-245.

———*Land and People of Indian States and Union Territories* : Madhya Pradesh. Volume 15. pp. 498-510.

Chatterji, Suniti Kumar (1966). *The People, Language and Culture of Orissa.* Bhubaneswar : Orissa Sahitya Academy.

Cohen, Abner (1947). *Urban Ethnicity.* London : Tavistock Publications.

Choudhary, Bidut Kumari (1999). *Odissi Dance,* Part-I, Bhubaneswar.

Dundes, A. (1965). *The Study of Folklore.* Englewood Cliff : Prentice Hall, p. 2.

Dash, Behari Kunja (1991). *Folklore of Orissa.* Bhubaneswar : Orissa Sahitya Academy.

Government of Orissa (2001). *District Statistical Handbook of Kalahandi,* Bhubaneswar, Directorate of Economic and Statistics.

———(1997). *Statistical Outline of Orissa.* Bhubaneswar : Director of Economic and Statistics.

———(2002). *Orissa Review,* Loksampark Bhawan : Bhubaneswar.

———(1980). *Orissa District Gazetteers.* Kalahandi : Bhubaneswar.

Government of India (1997 to 2002). *Approach Paper to the Ninth Five Year Plan.* Planning Commission. New Delhi : Government of India.

Goswami, Praphulladatta (1976). *Songs and Tales of North East India.* Guwahati : The Folklore Society of Assam.

Gupta, S.P. Krishnalal and Mahua Bhattacharya (2002). *Cultural Tourism in India.* New Delhi : Indraprastha Museum of Art and Archaeology.

Hasnain, Nadeem (2007). *Tribal India.* Lucknow : New Royal Book Company.

Indira Gandhi National Open University (2004). TS-1 : *Foundation Course in Tourism : Tourism Phenomenon,* New Delhi.

Janah, Sunil (1993). *The Tribals of India,* Delhi : Oxford University Press.

Kumar, Sanjay (2002). *The Heroic Dance—Ghumra.* Kalahandi : Bhawanipatna.

Kuanra, Durgacharana (1994). *Mayurbhanja Chhau Nritya.* Bhubaneswar : Orissa Sahitya Academy.

Mahapatra, K.H. (1997). *Tribal Language and Culture of Orissa.* Bhubaneswar : Academy of Tribal Dialect and Culture.

Mahapatra, Santanu (2000). Forewords. *Rangabhumi Bisesanka* : Bhubaneswar.

Munasingh, Mohan and McNelly, Jeffrey (1994). *Sustainable Tourism Development in Protected Area Economics and Policy.* Ed. By Kathryn Lawrence. Washington DC : World Conservation Union.

Mahanti, K.K. and A.C. Shaoo (2000). Aspects of Ethnomusicology of the Tribes of Orissa. *Banaja* : Academy of Tribal Dialects and Culture. pp. 22-23.

Nayak, P.K. (2000). *The Voice of Silence, Sonepur Durbar and Indian Cultural Traditions.* Bhubaneswar : Sahitya Academy. pp. 34-41.

Narayan, Leilla (1989). *Ethnicity in Urban Context.* Jaipur : Rawat Publications.

Oomen, T.K. (2001). *Citizenship, Nationality and Ethnicity.* New Delhi : Replika Press.

Orissa Sangeet Natak Akademi (2000). *Rangabhumi Bisesanka.* Bhubaneswar (Orissa).

———(1997). *Lokanrutya Bisesanka.* Bhubaneswar (Orissa).

———(1998). *Orissa Lokanrutya.* Bhubaneswar (Orissa).

Panda, Bhawanisankar (1999). *Kalahandi Itihasa*. The First Chronological History of Kalahandi Ex-State District. Bhawanipatna : Sanskrutika Publication.

Pasayat, Chitrasen (1998). *Tribe, Caste and Folk Culture*. Jaipur : Rawat Publications.

— — — (2003). *Glimpses of Tribal and Folk Culture*. New Delhi : Anmol Publications.

Prasad, Ramakanta (1988). *Tribes : A Study in Cultural Ecology and Tribal Dynamics of the Parahiya*. Delhi : Amar Prakashan.

Pattnaik, D.N. (2000). *Folk Dances of Orissa*. Bhubaneswar : Sangeet Natak Academy.

Panigrahi, M.R. (1998). *Odishara Lokanritya*. Bhubaneswar : Sangeet Natak Academy.

Ray, Aditya. and B.V. Sharma (2005). *Dimensions of Researches in Indian Anthropology*. Allahabad : The Oriental Institute of Cultural and Social Research.

Redfield, Robert (1947). The Folk Society. *The American Journal of Sociology*. Vol. 52 (4). pp. 293-308.

Samal, Kishore Chandra (2002). *Impact of Economic Reform (Liberalisation, Globalisation and Privatisation) on Industrial Sector Including Small Scale Enterprises and Informal Sector*. Moscow and Bhubaneswar : NKCDS.

Singh, K.S. (1990). *Ethnicity, Identity and Development*. New Delhi : Manohar Publications. pp. 31-41.

Senapati, Nilamani and D.C. Kaur (1981). *Gazetteer of Kalahandi District*, Bhubaneswar, Department of Revenue, Government of Orissa (1968). *Gazetteer of Bolangir District*, Government Press, Calcutta.

———(1971) *Gazetteer of Sambalpur District*, Government Press, Calcutta.

Sharma, Manorama (1999). *Music India*. New Delhi : A.P.H. Publishing Corporation.

Shibakar, Mehar (2003). *Self-Help Group and Power in Orissa*. Bhubaneswar : NKCDS.

Seegar, Charles (1980). *www.wikipedia.org*

Tamo, Mibang and Sarati K. Chanduri (2004). *Folk Culture and Oral Literature from North-East India*. New Delhi : Mittal Publications.

Thomas, William (1846). *www.wikipedia.org*

Tayenge, A. (1990). *Adi Folksong*. Director of Research, Itanagar : Government of Arunachal Pradesh.

Tisdell, Clem (1996). Ecotourism, Economics, and The Environment Observation. China : *Journal of Travel Research.*

Tiwari, Kapil (1993). *Pratyaya.* Bhopal : Madhya Pradesh Adivasi Lok Kala Parishad.

Vidyarthi, L.P. (1980). *Folklore : The Pulse of the People in the Context of Indian Folklore.* New Delhi : Concept Publishing Company.

World Trade Organisation, Facts and Figures. *www.world-tourism.org*

Index